LETTER TRACING

FOR PRESCHOOLERS AND TODDLERS

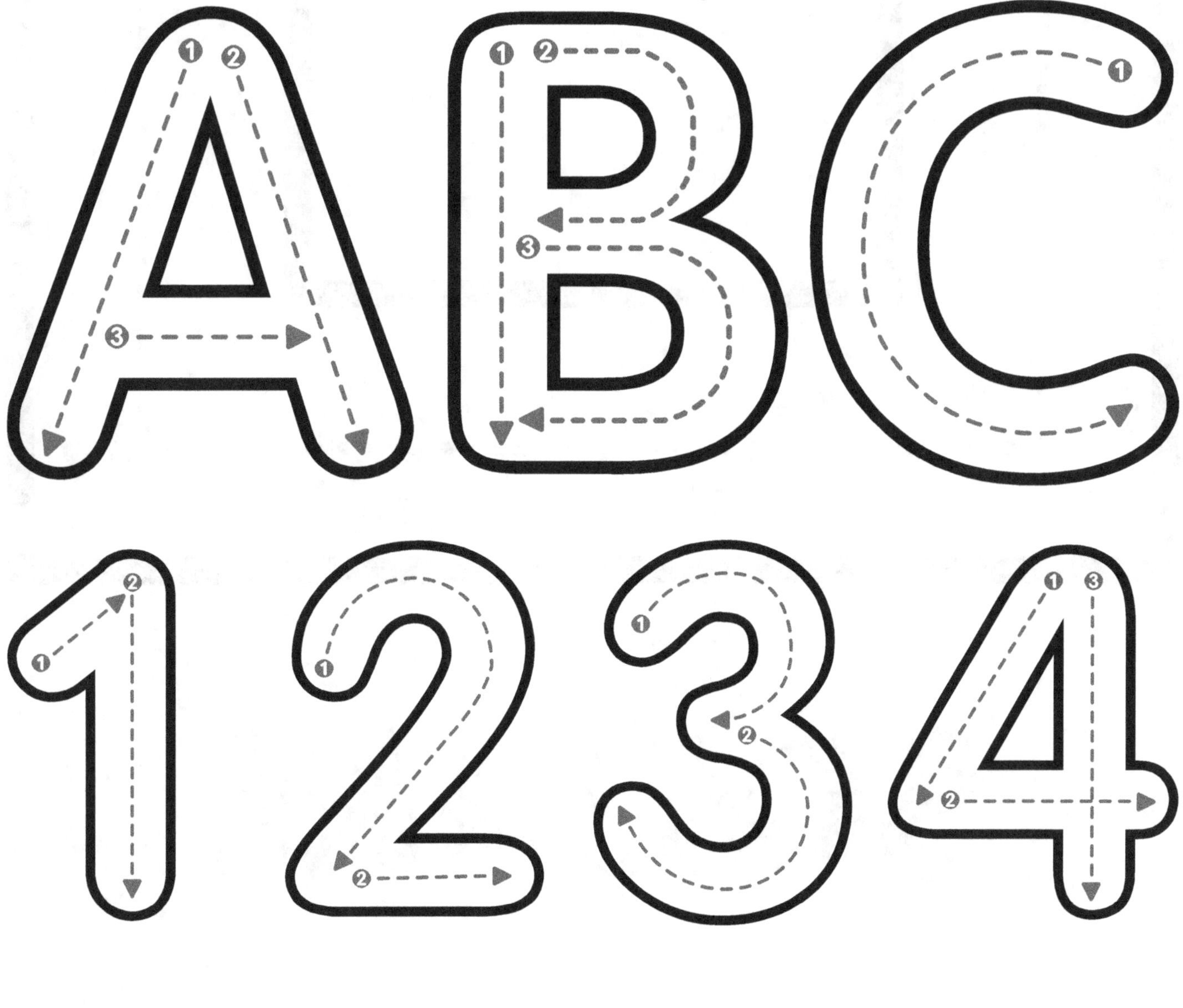

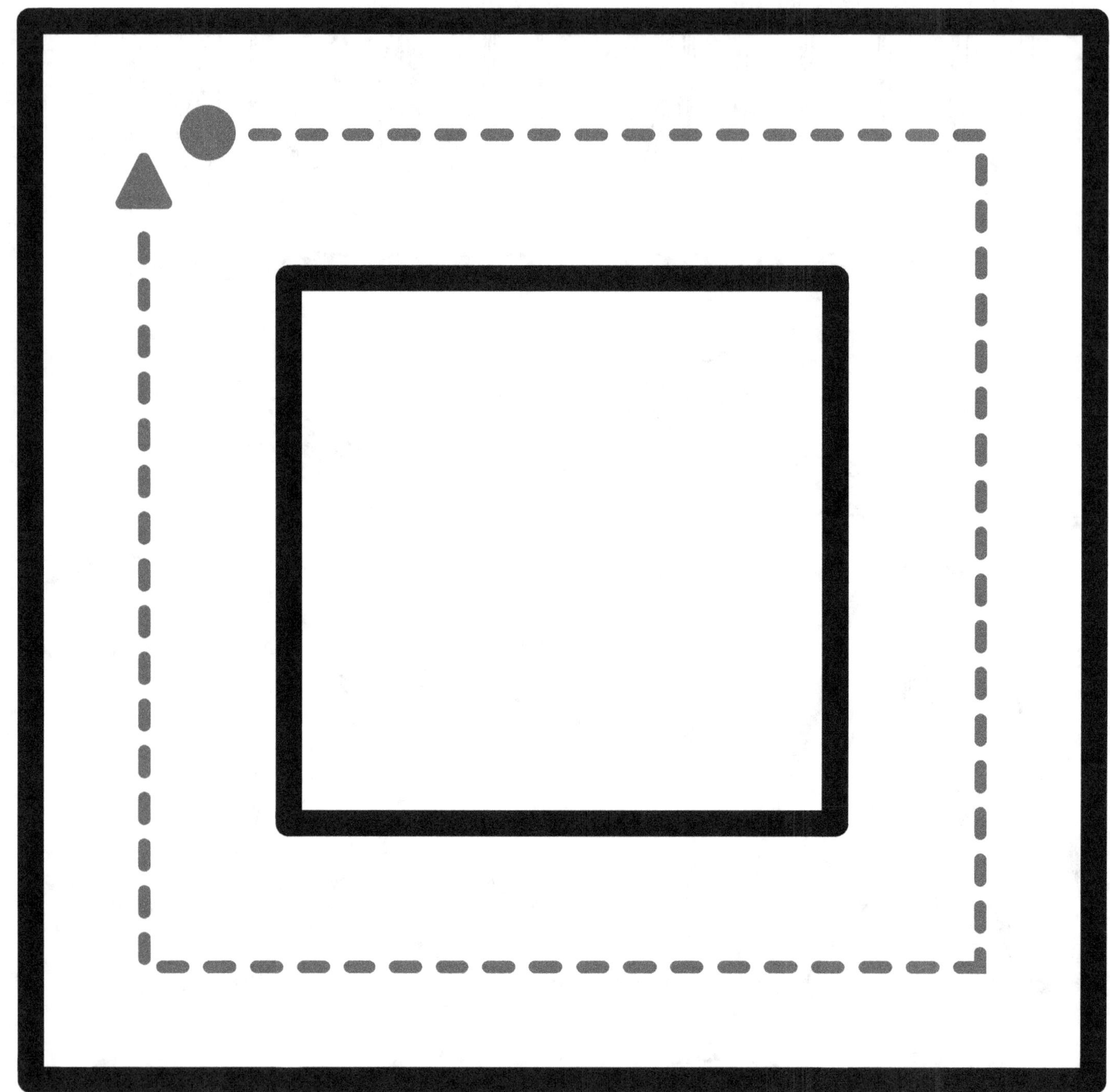

SQUARE

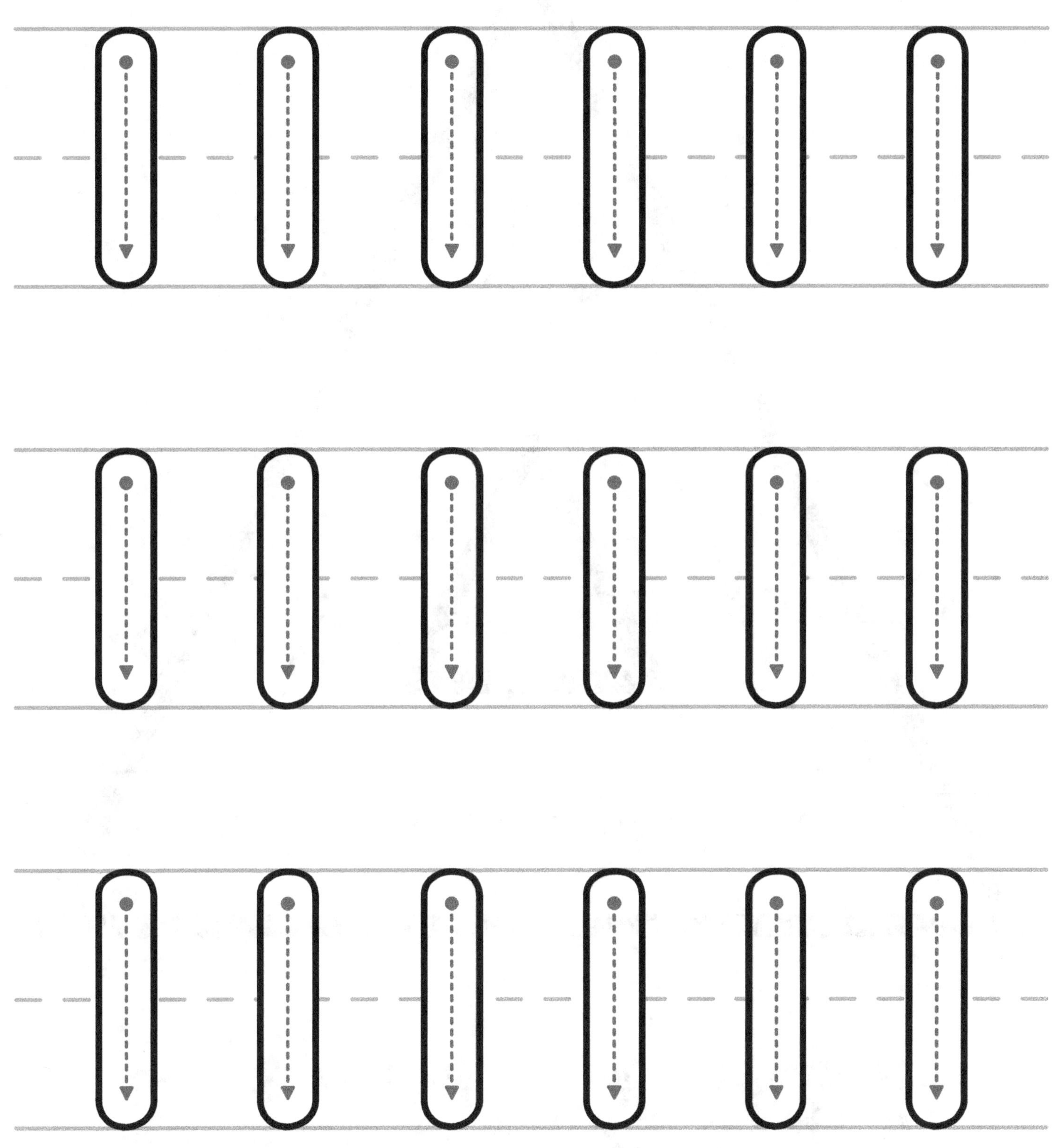

TRIANGLE

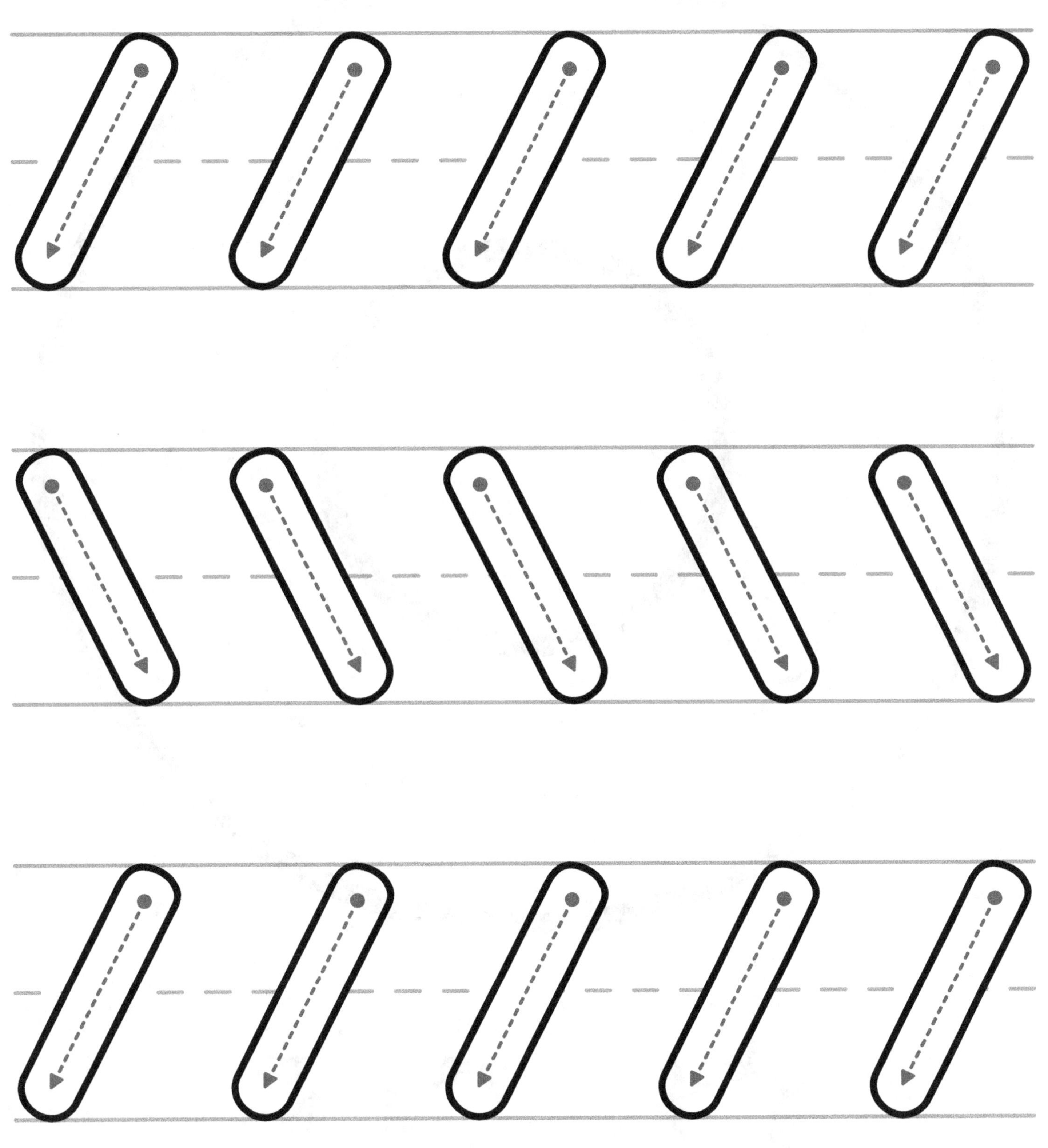

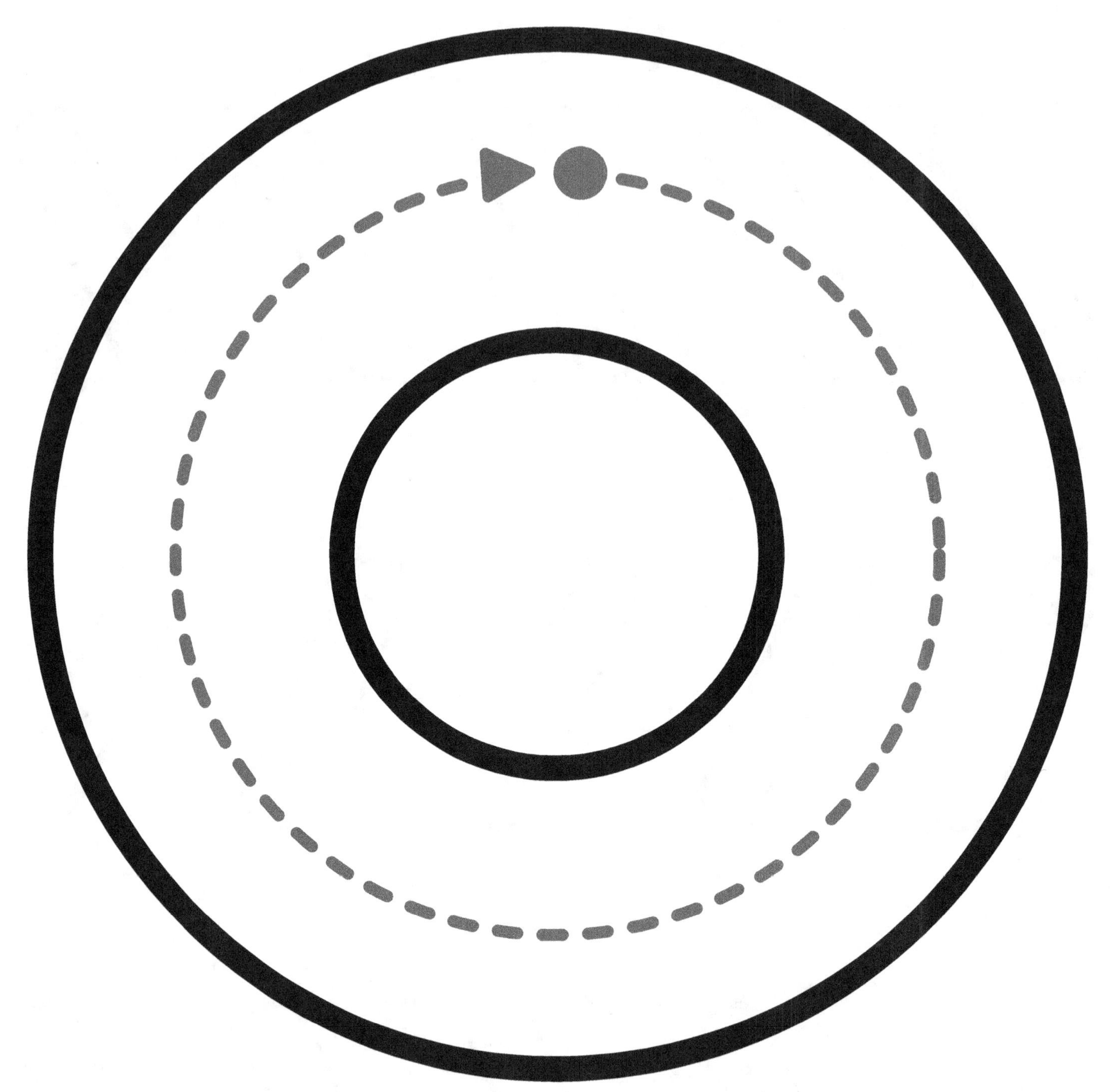

CIRCLE

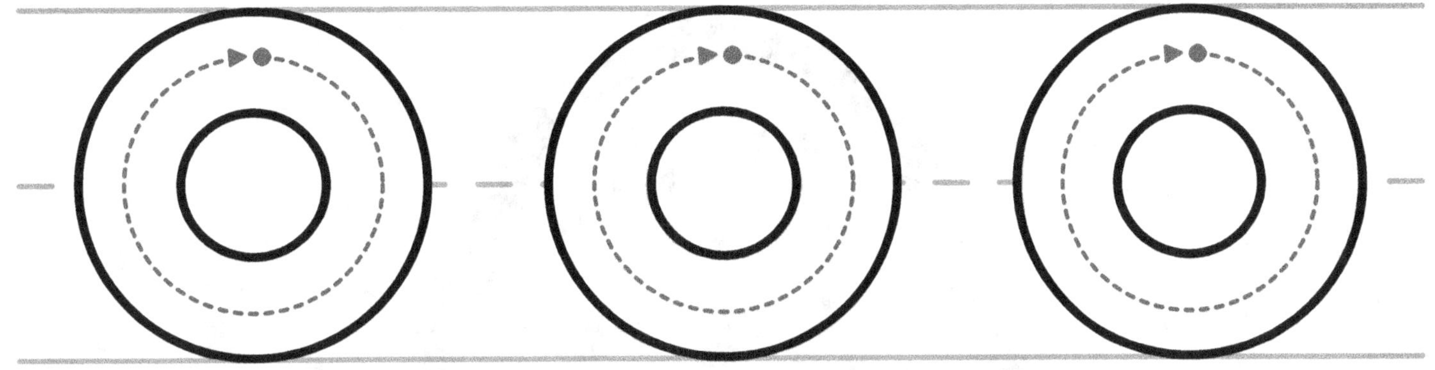

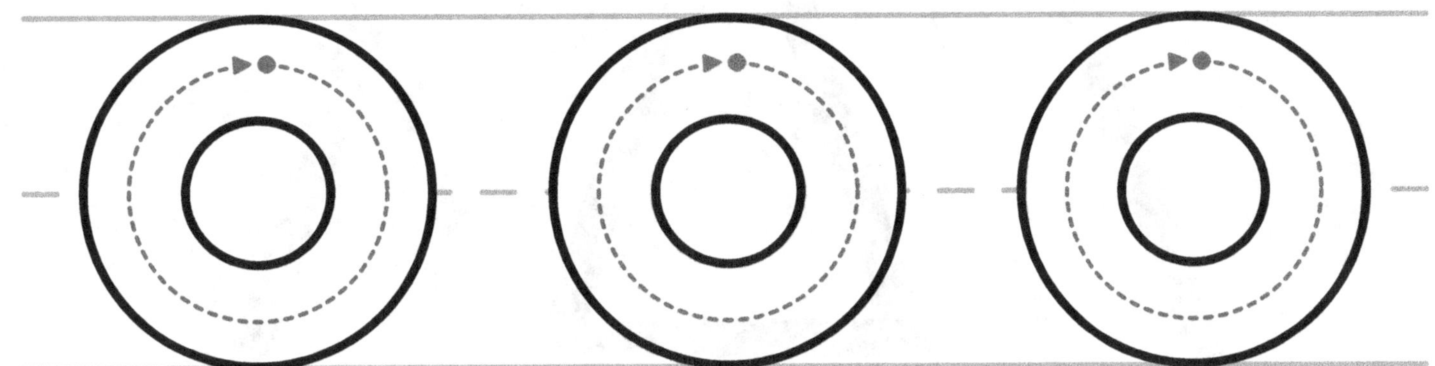

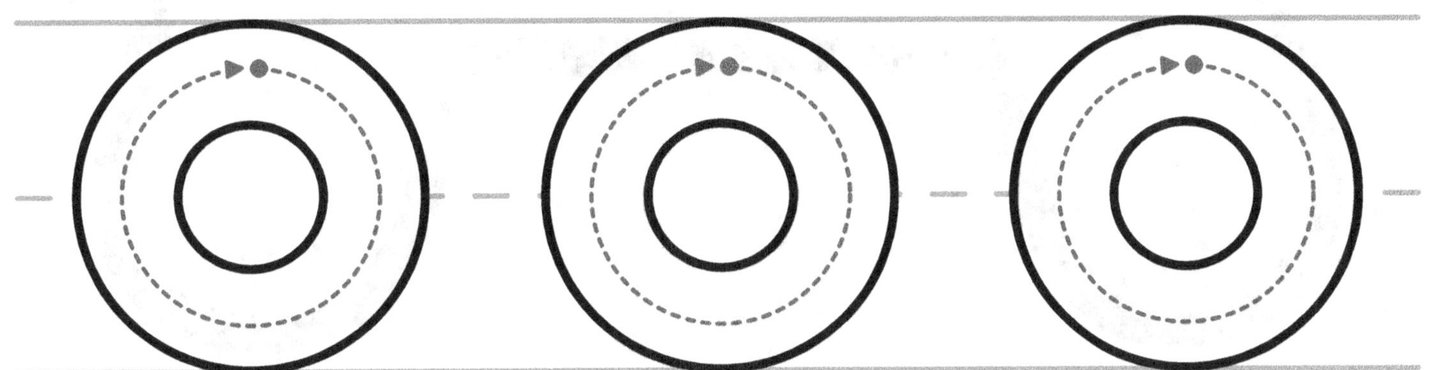

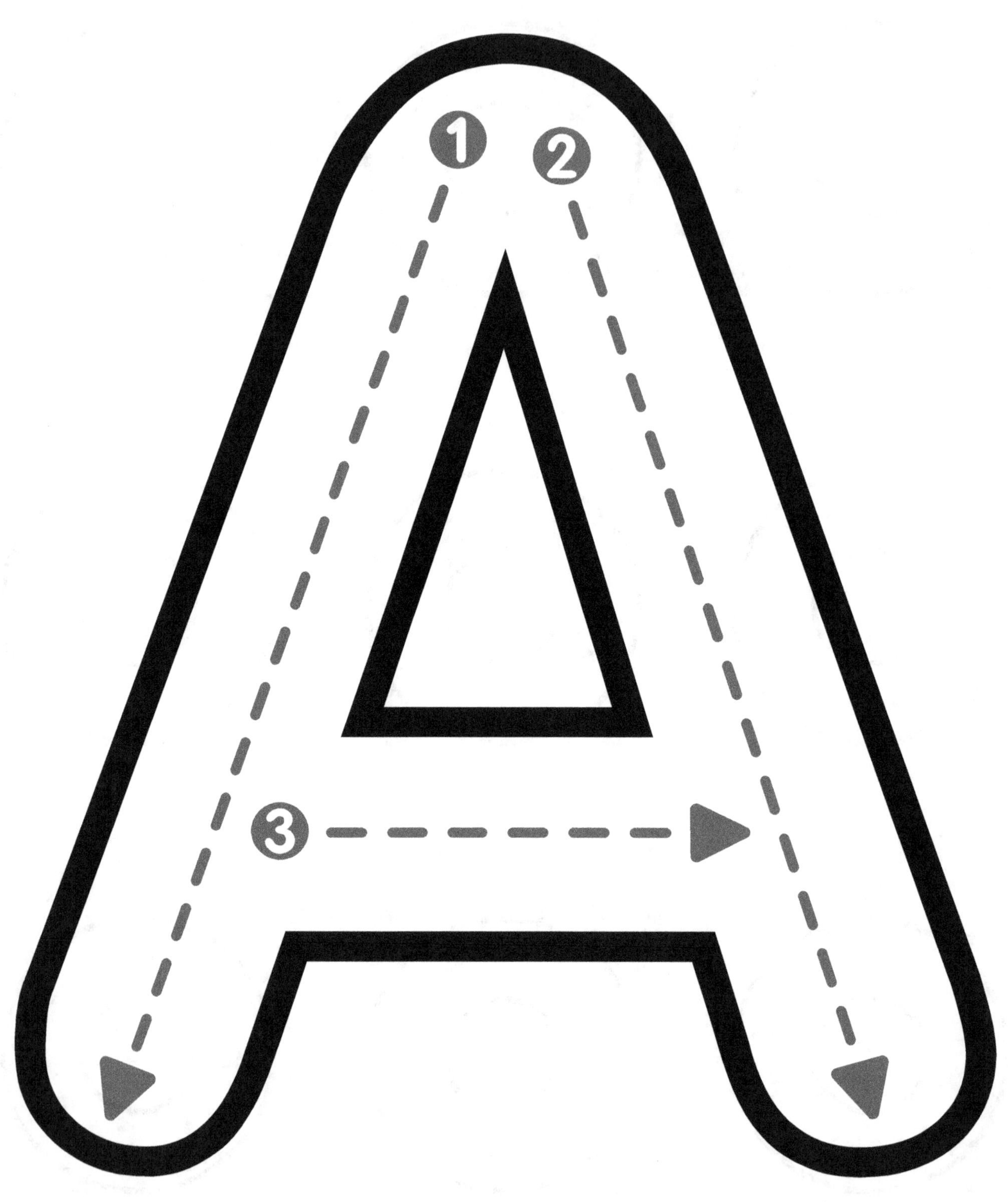
1
2
3

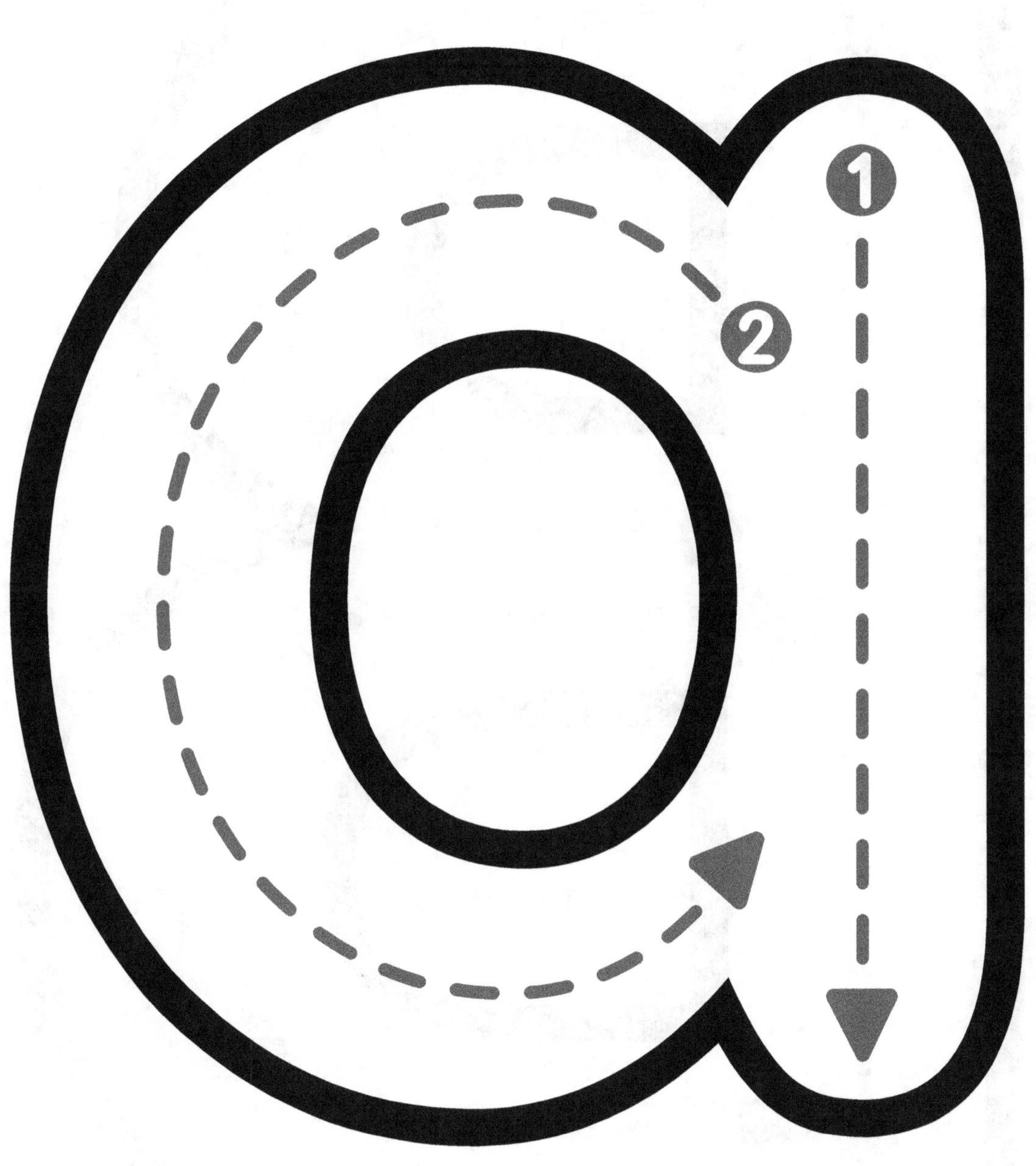

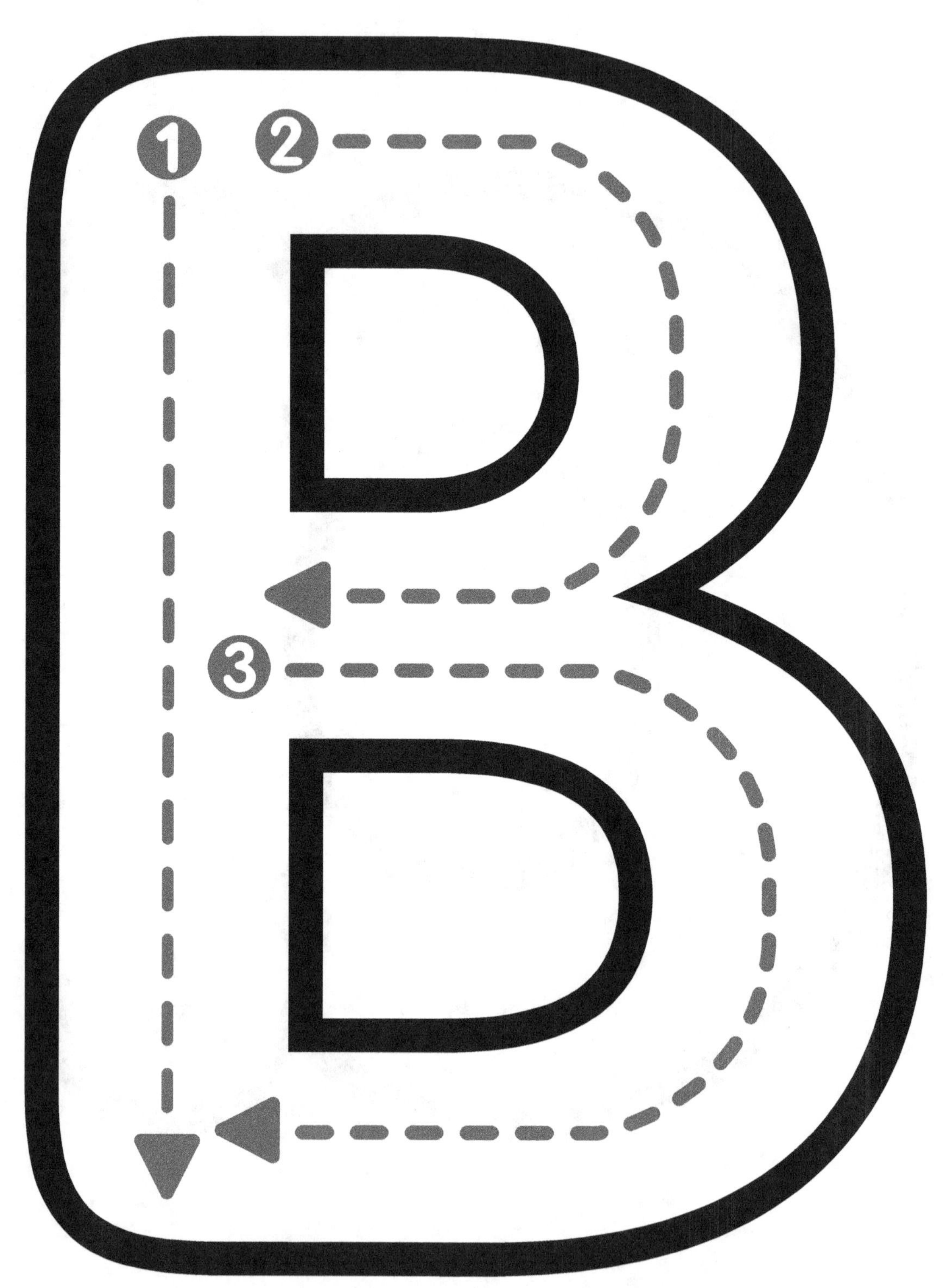

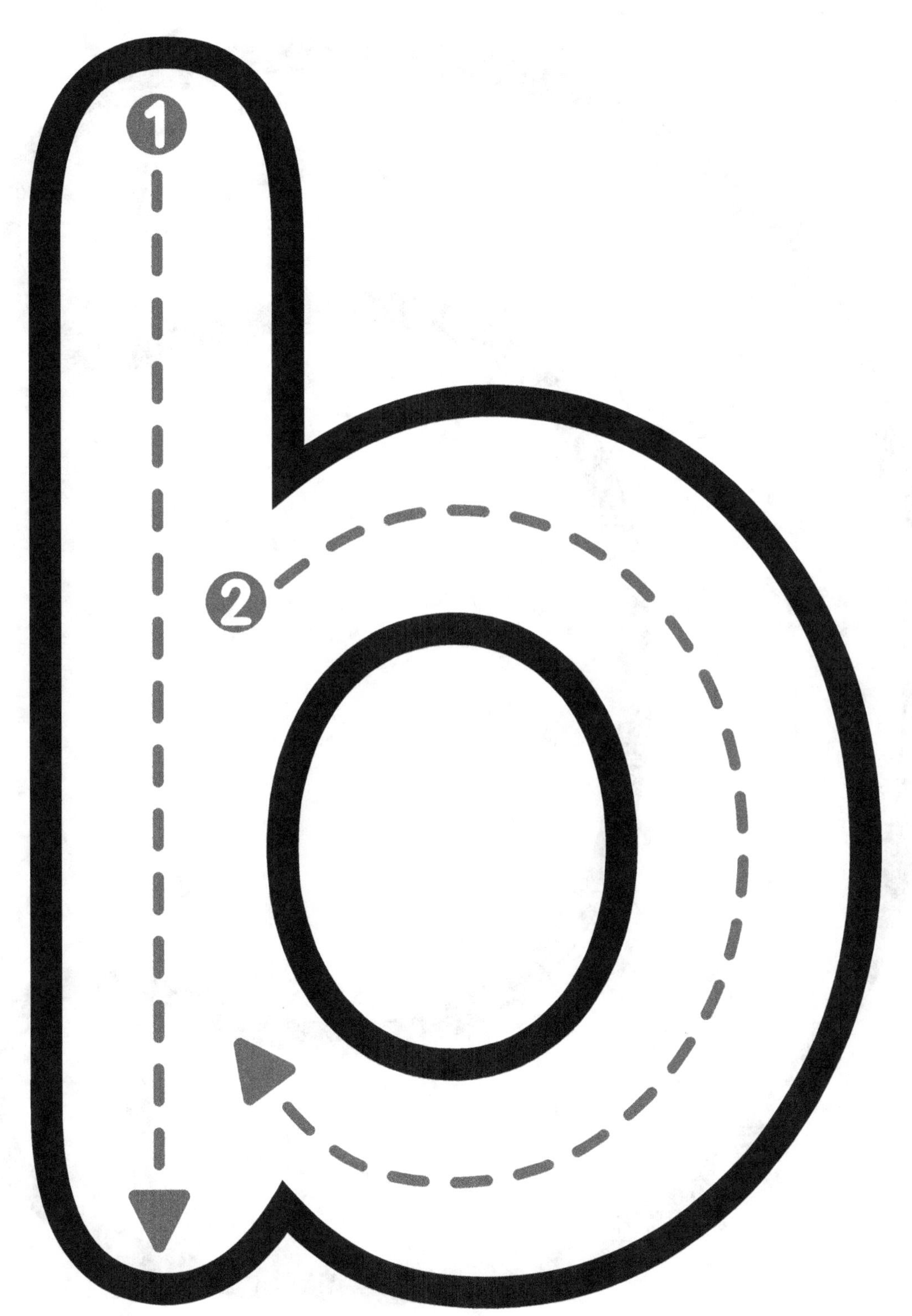

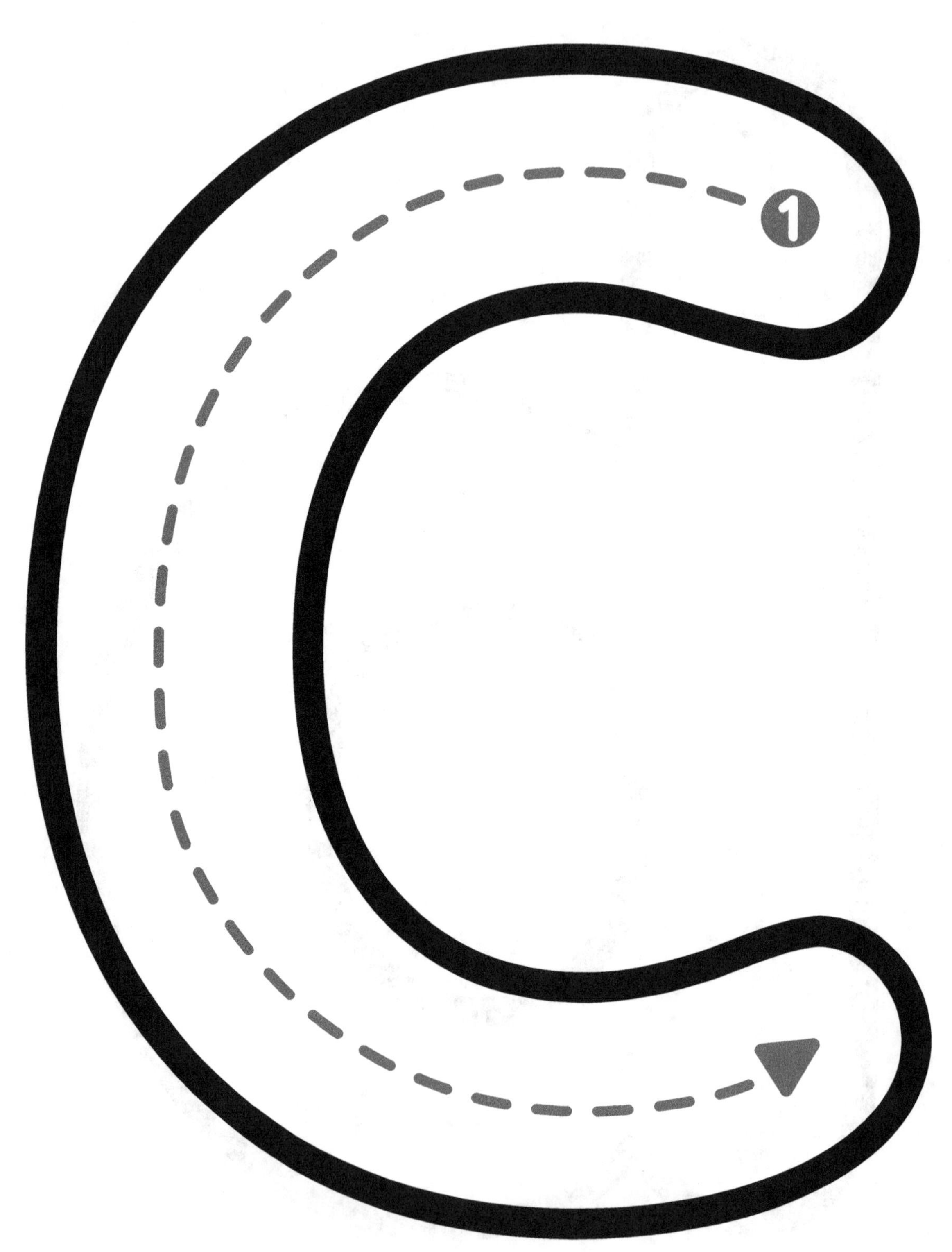

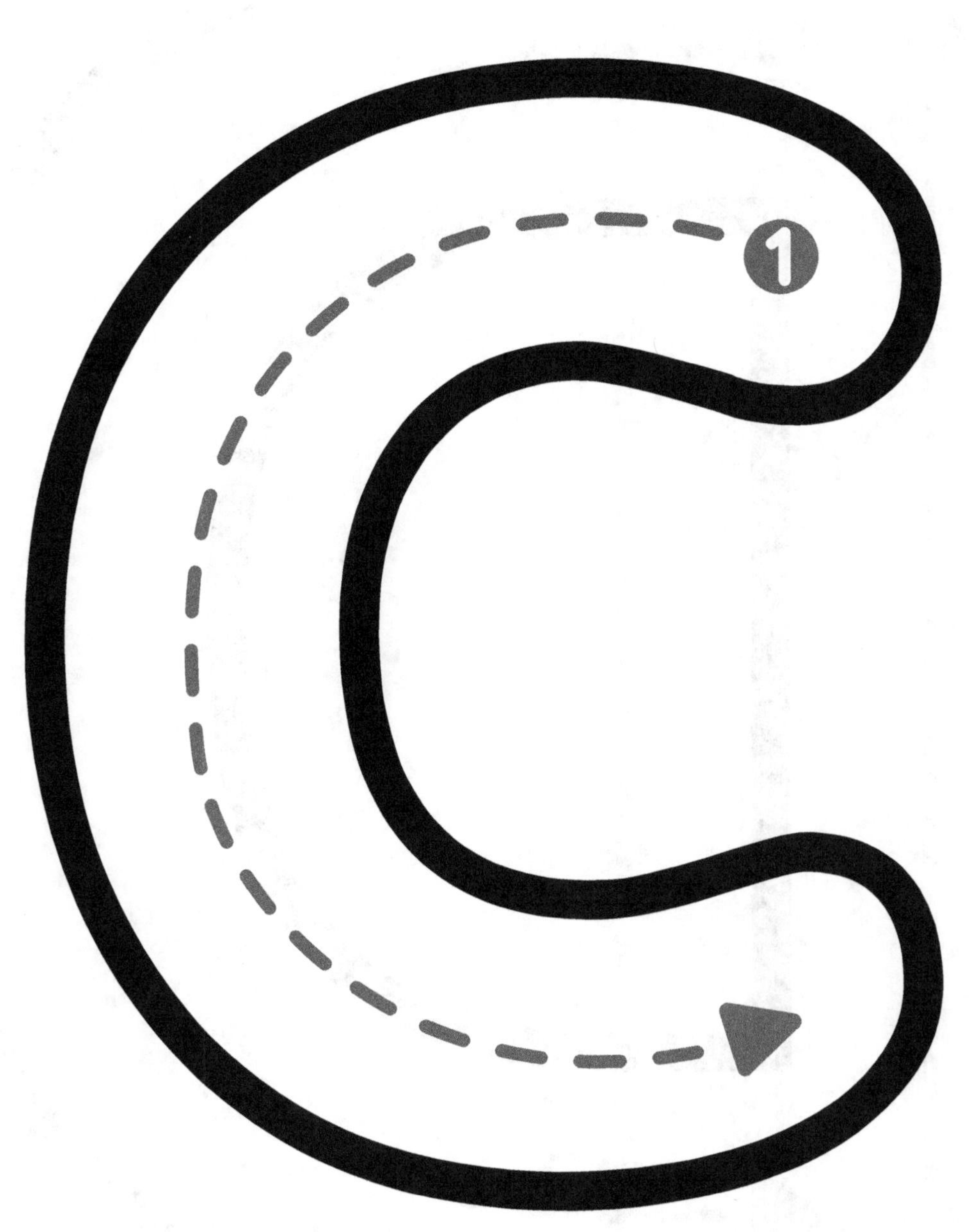

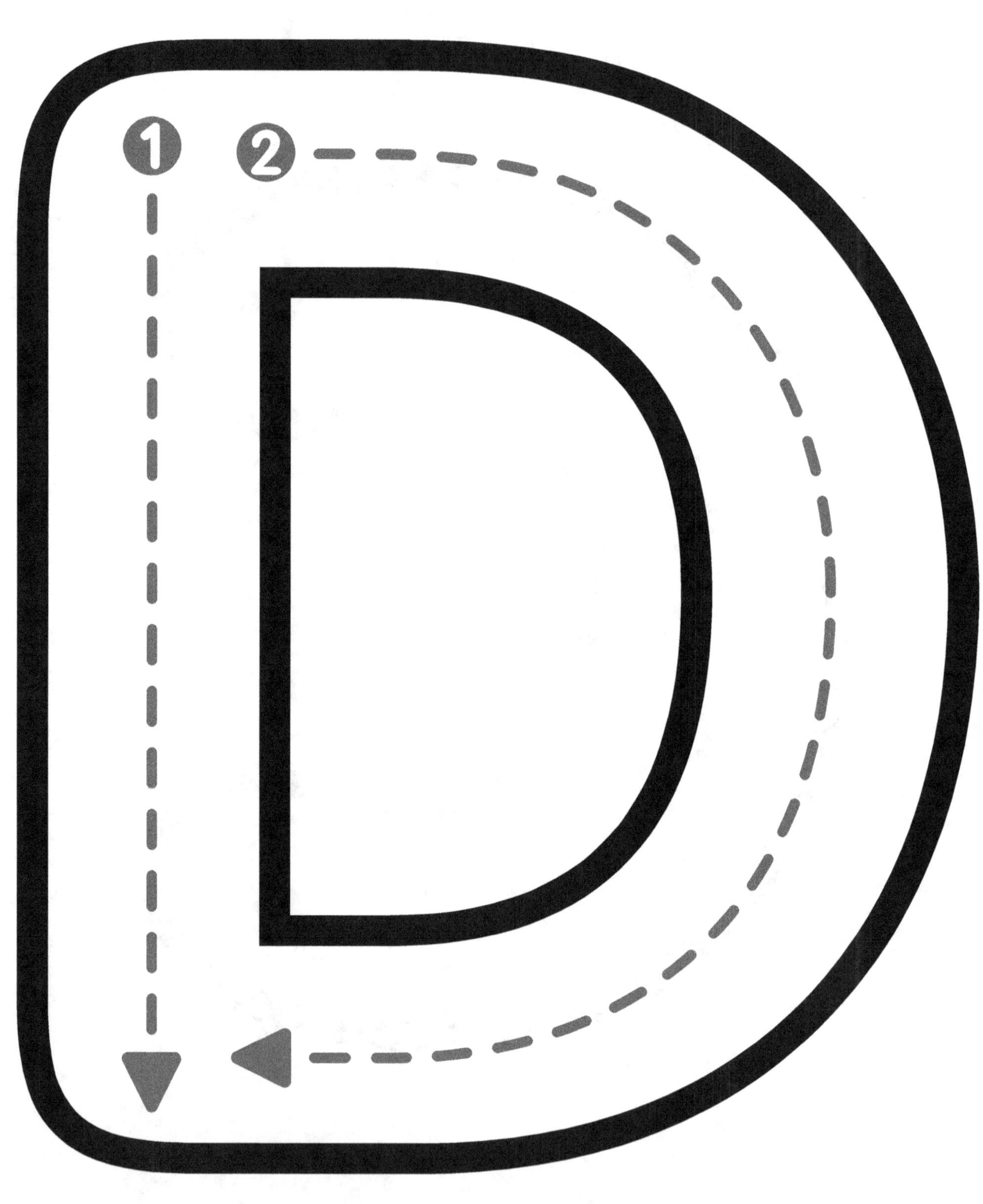
1
2

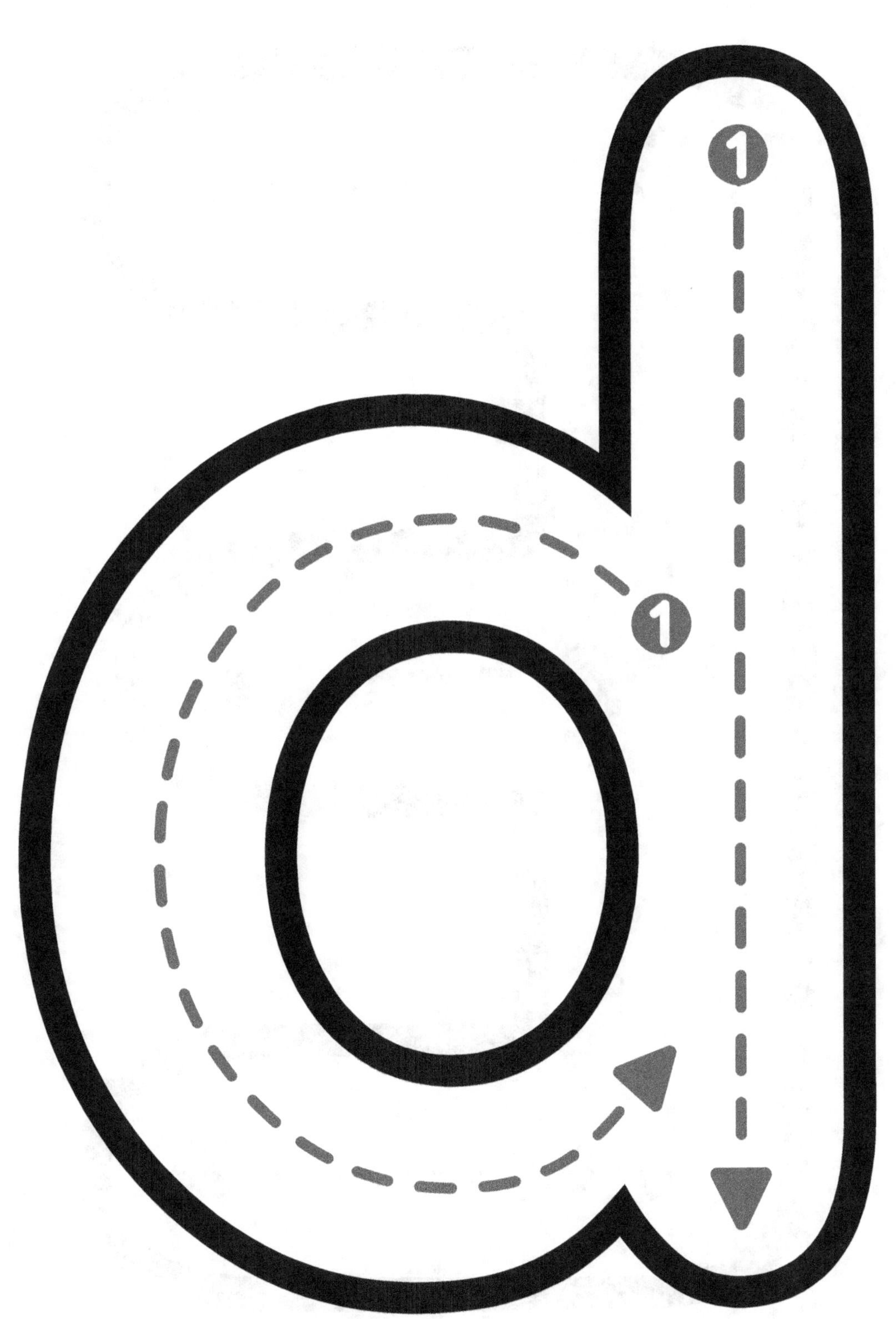

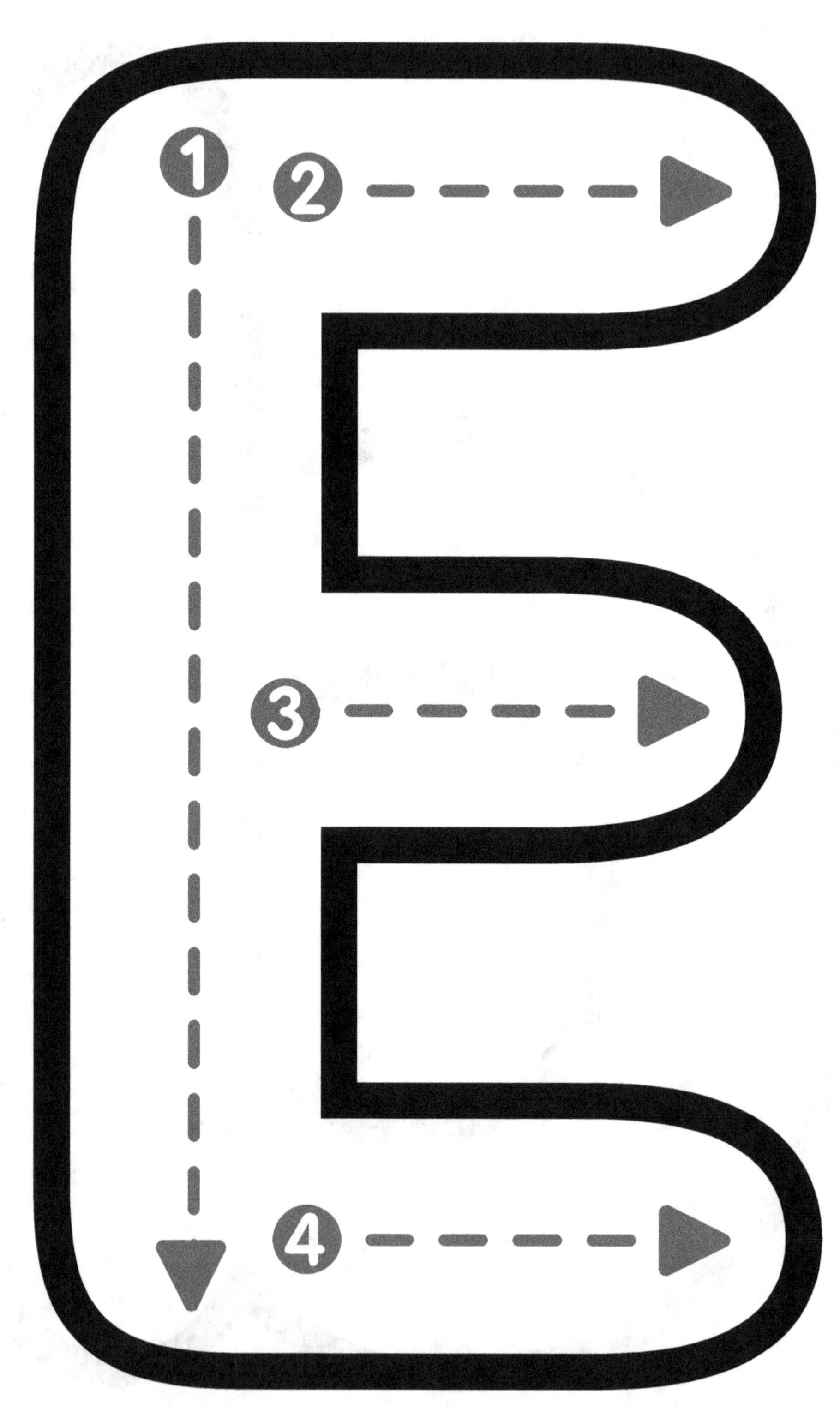

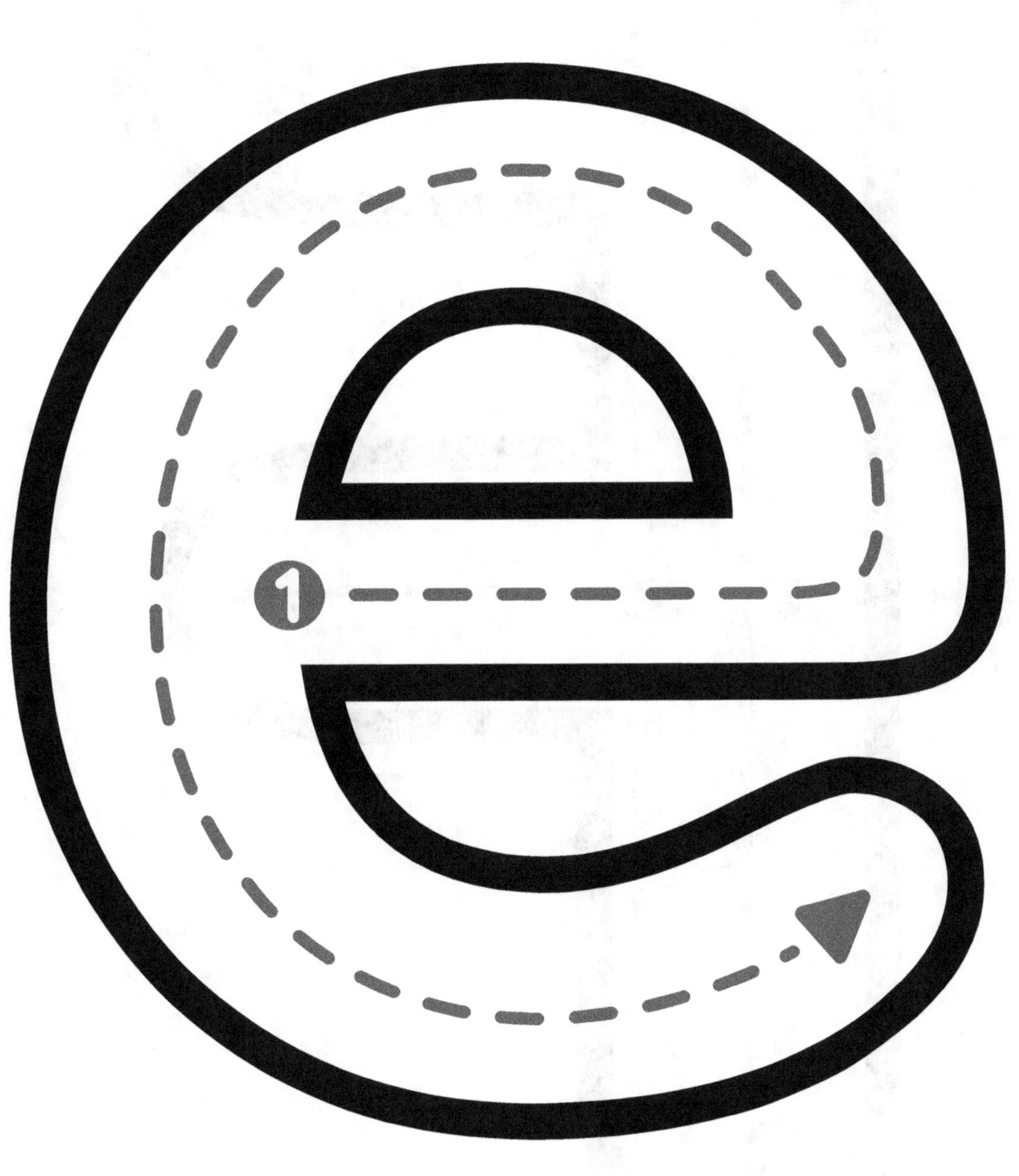

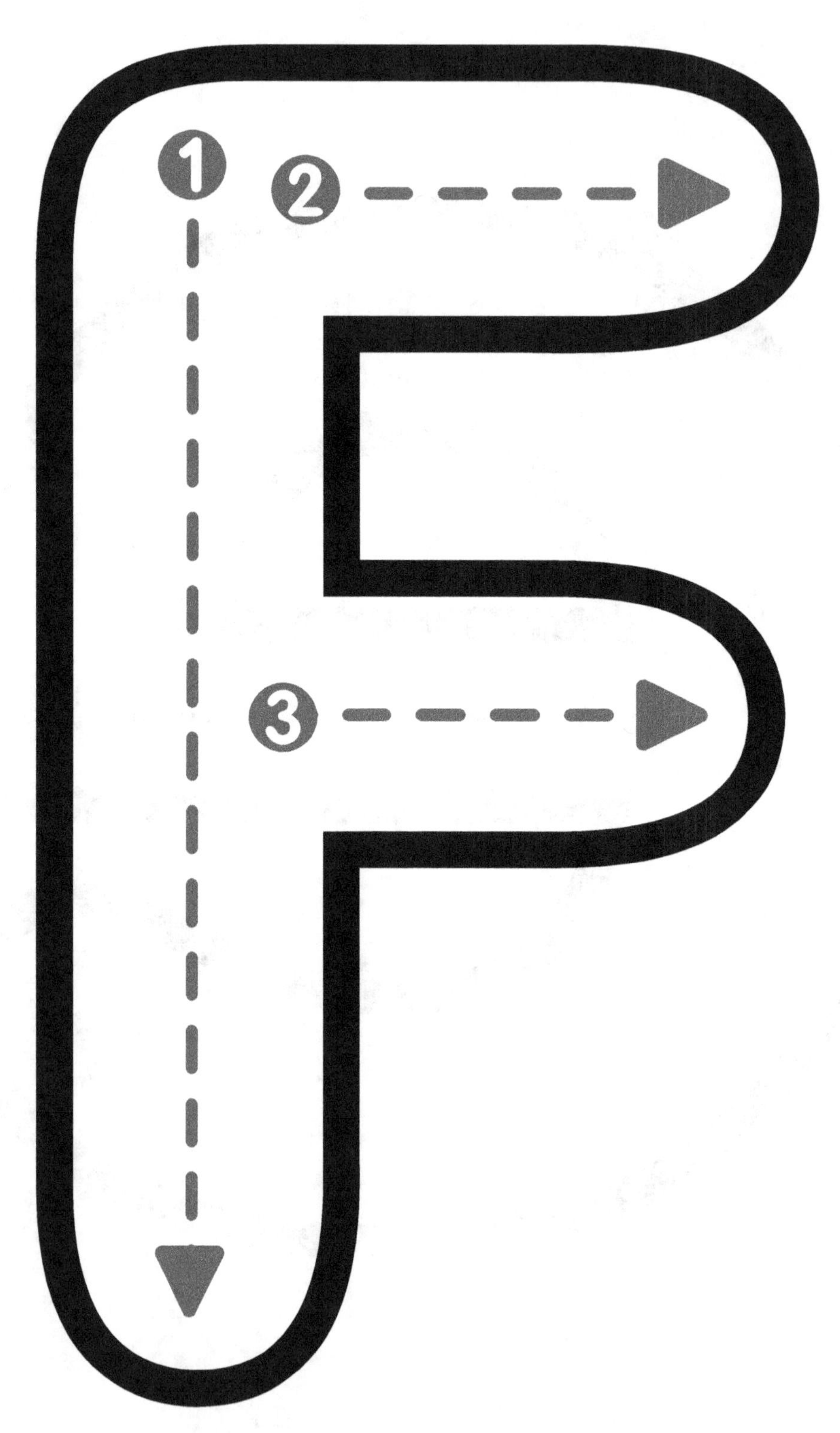

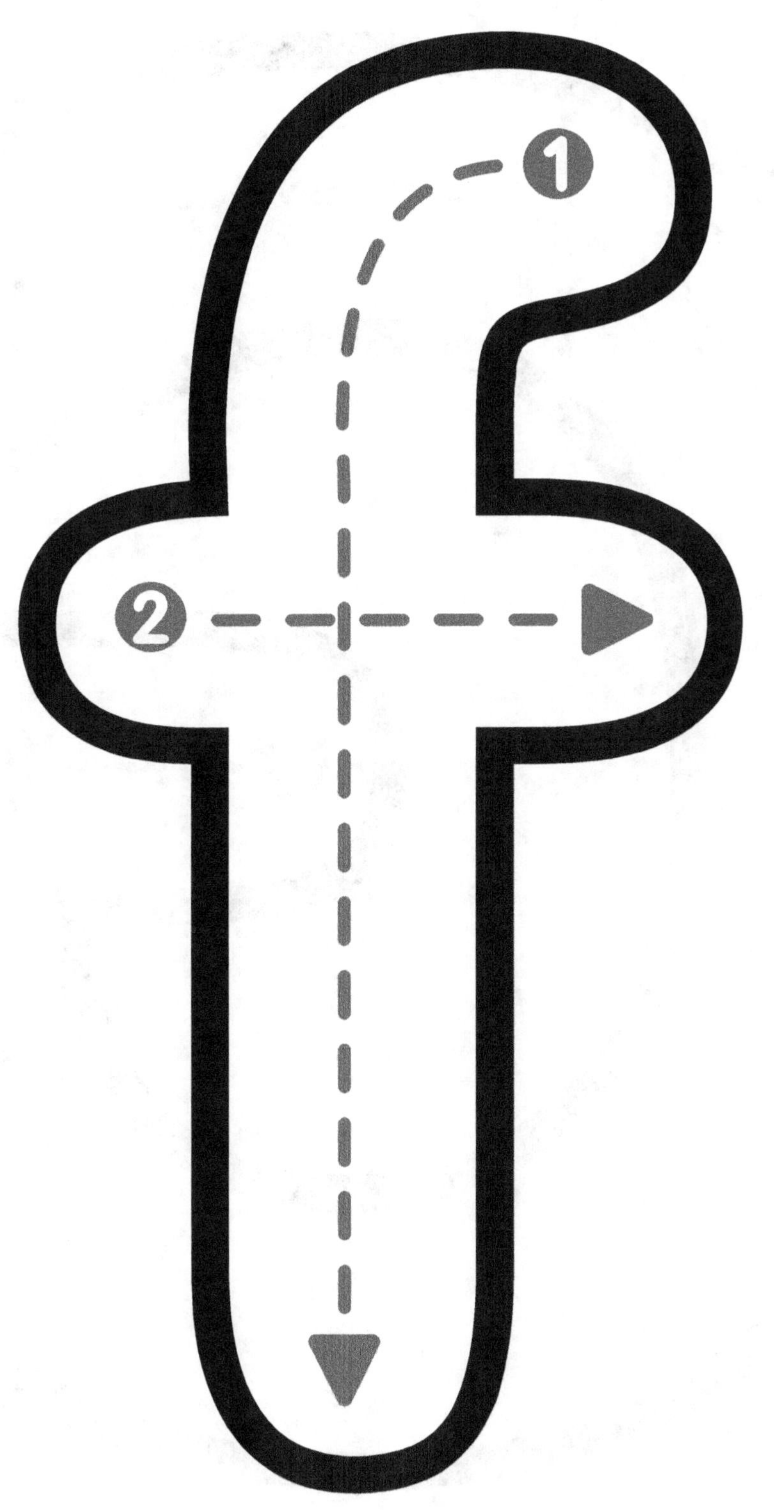

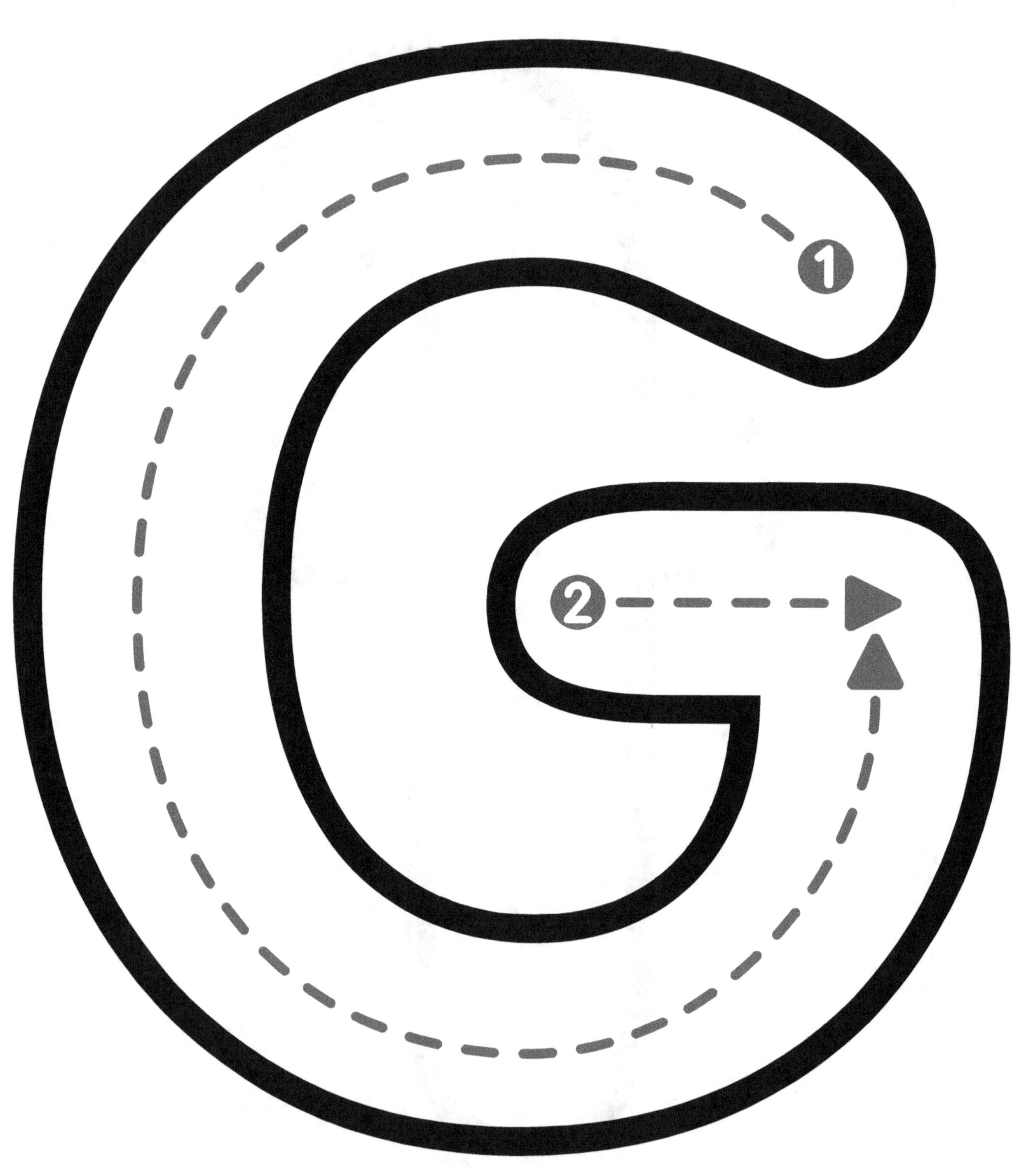
1
2

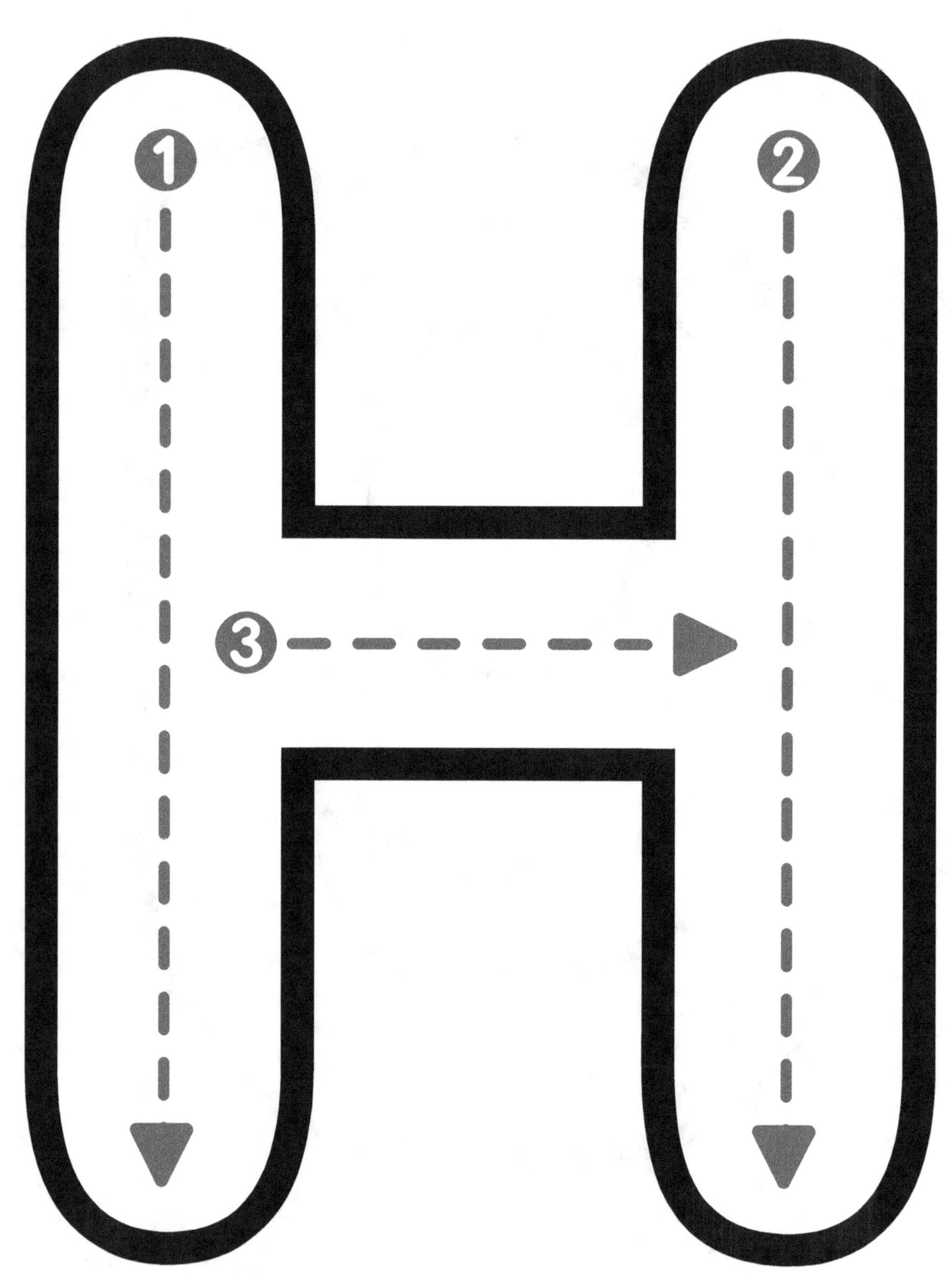

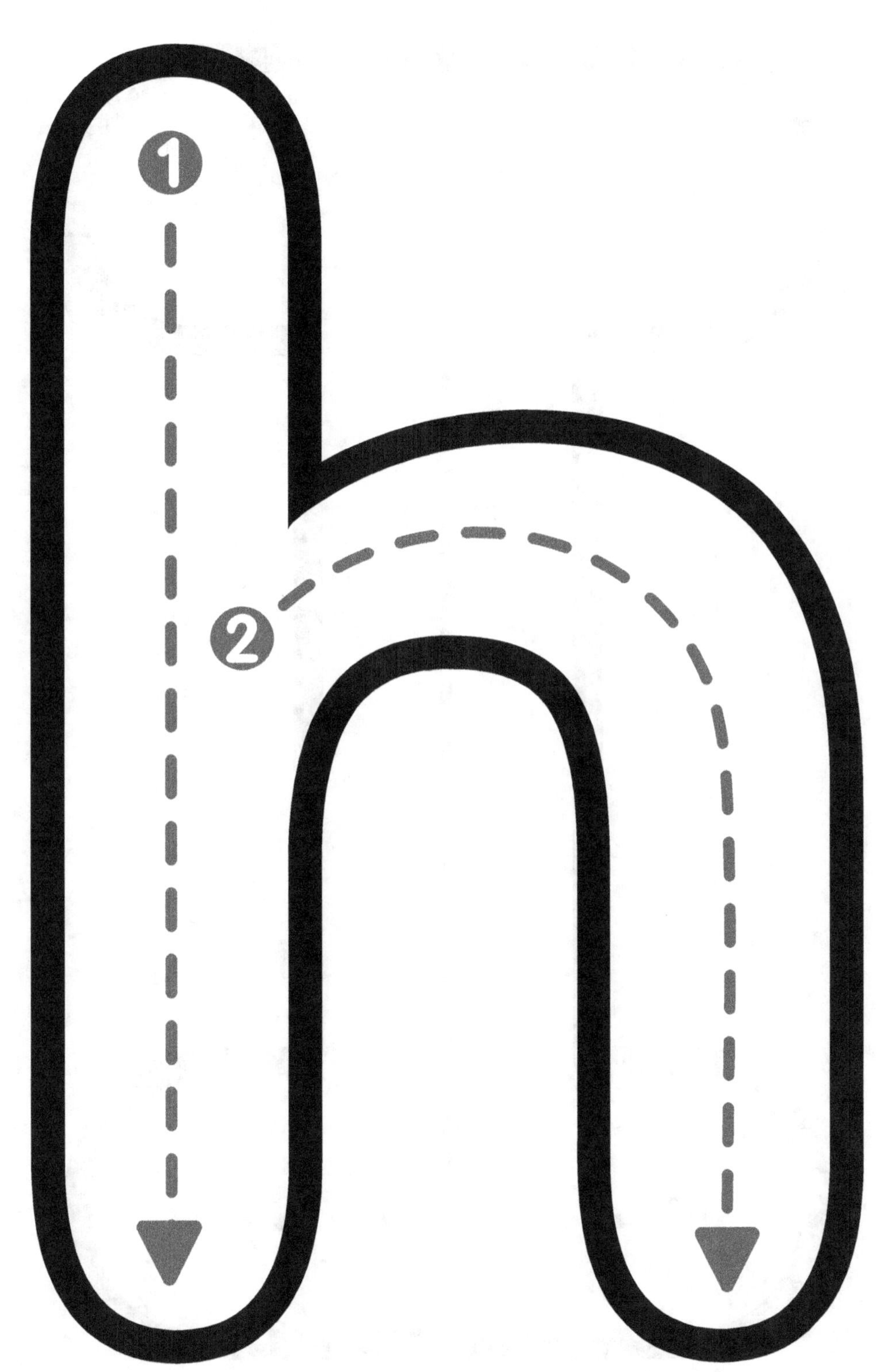

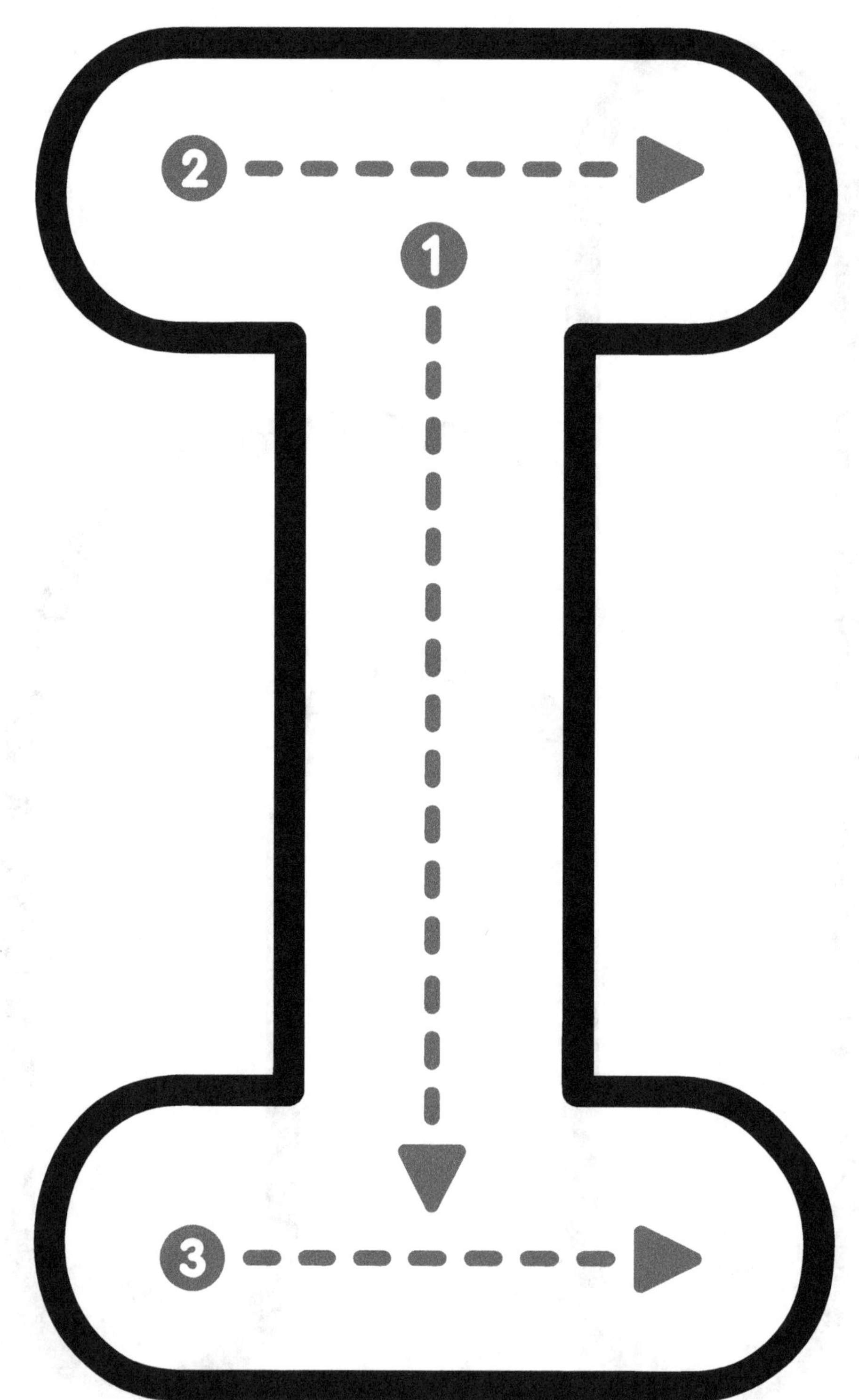

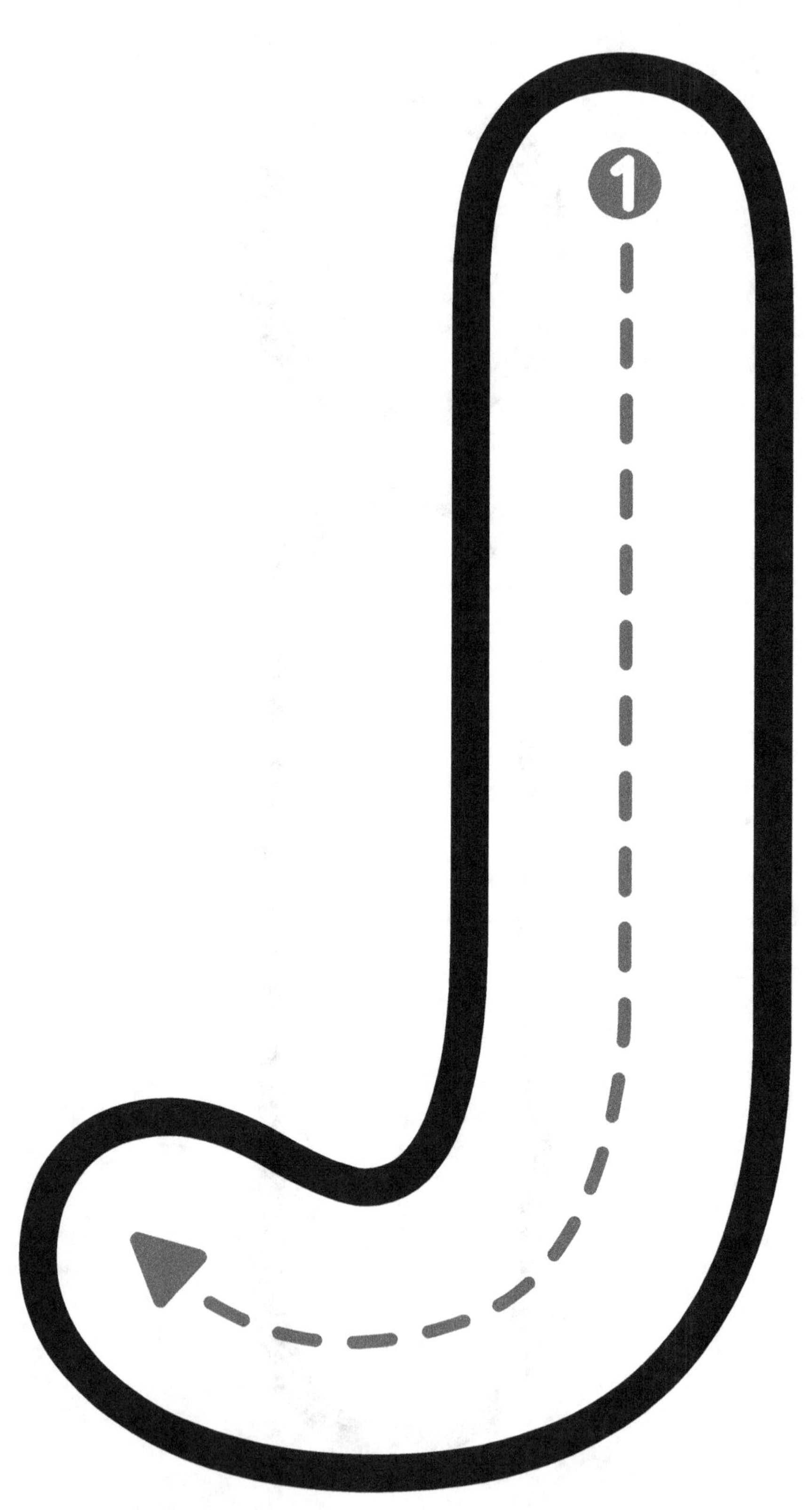
1

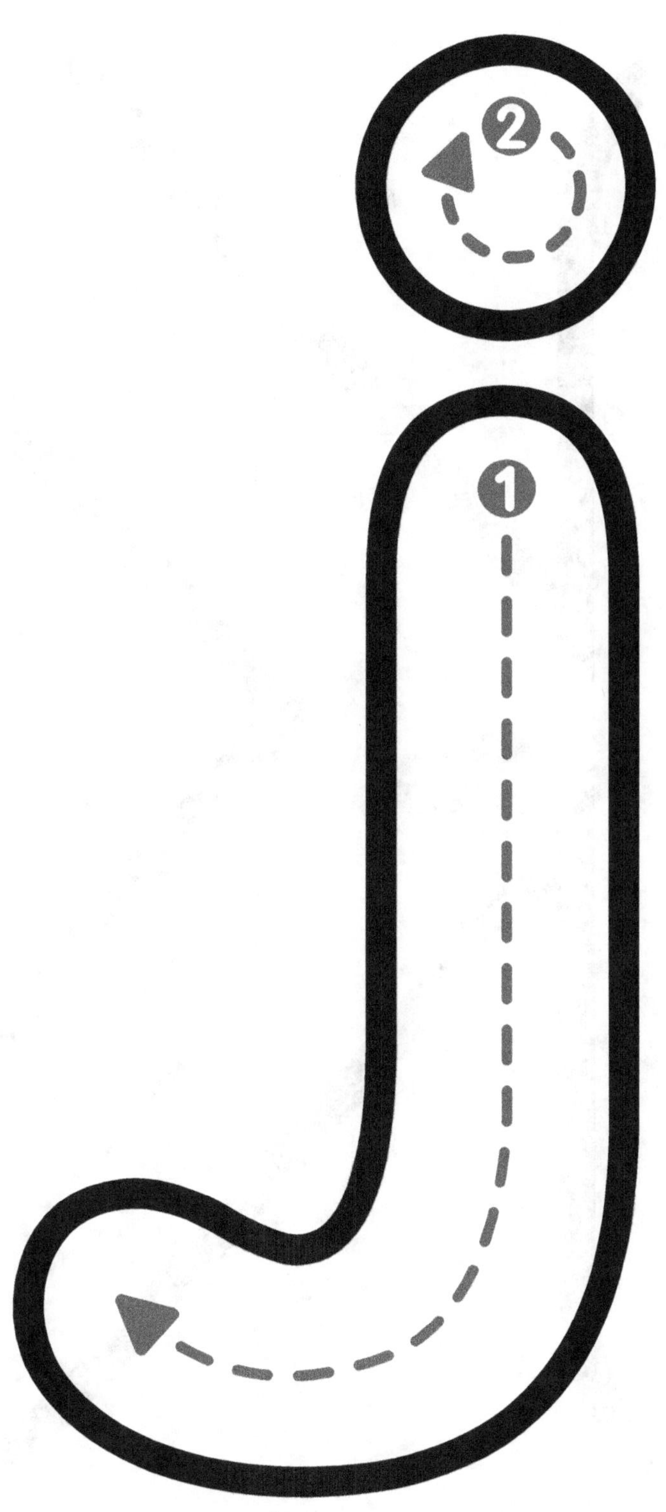

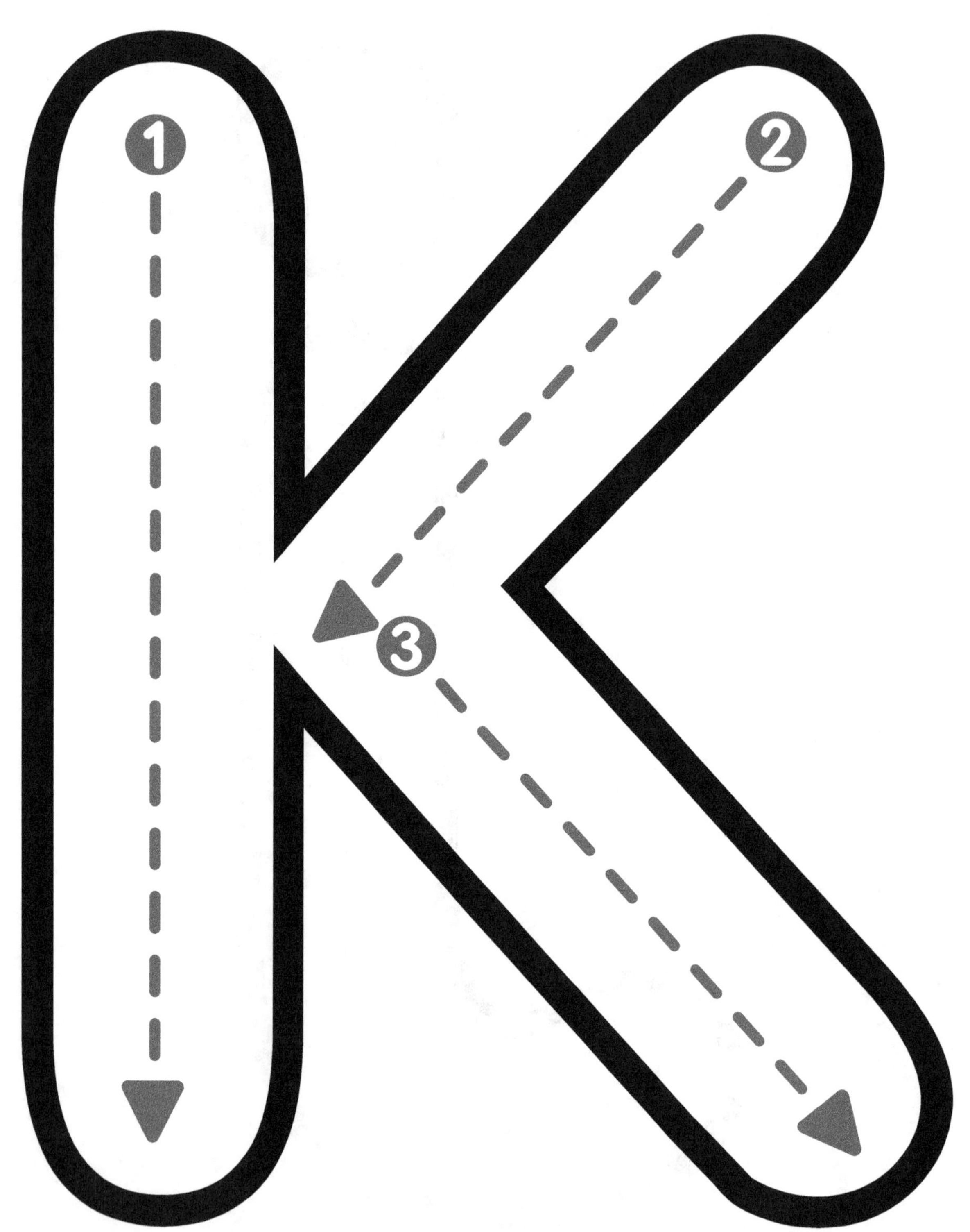

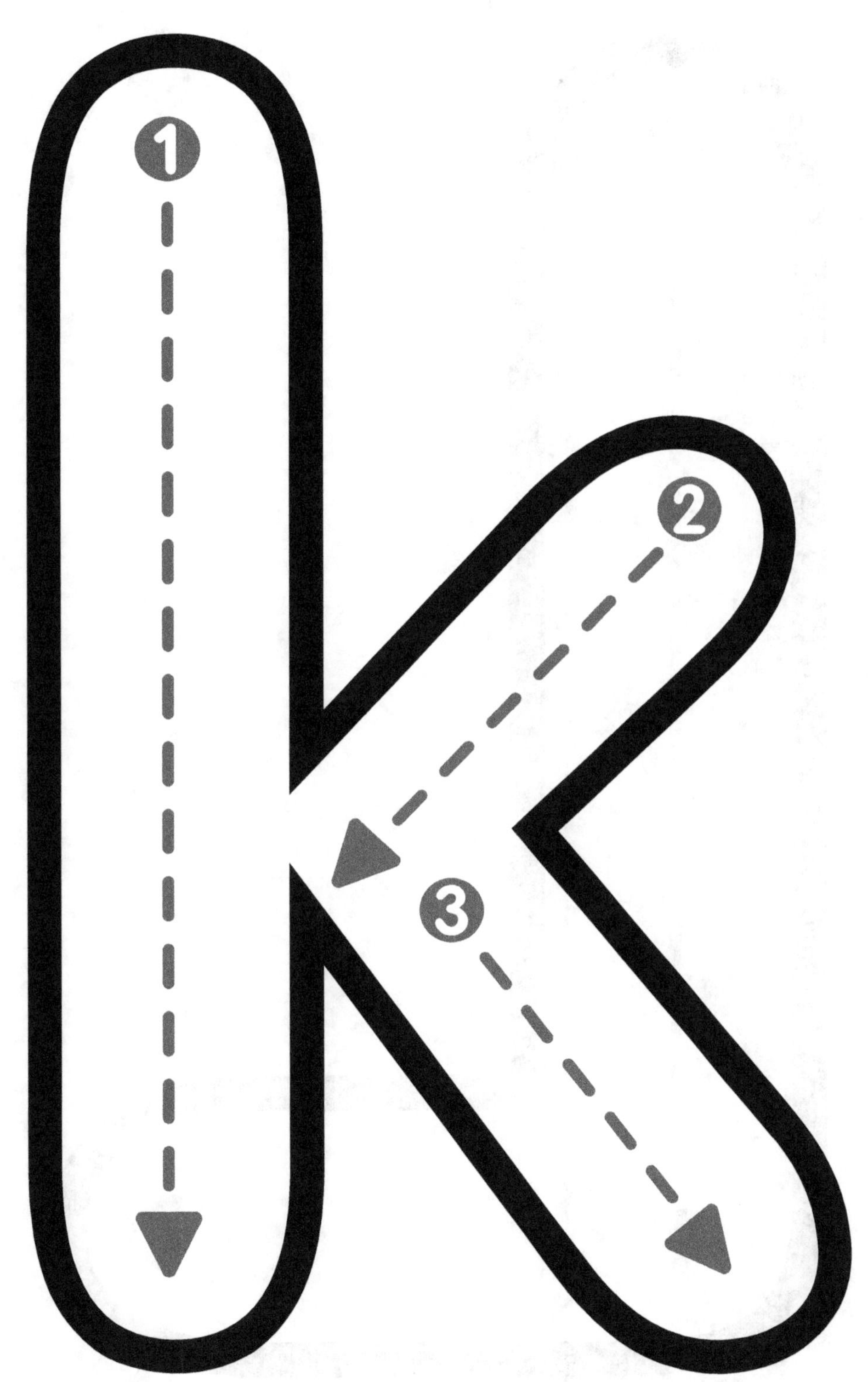

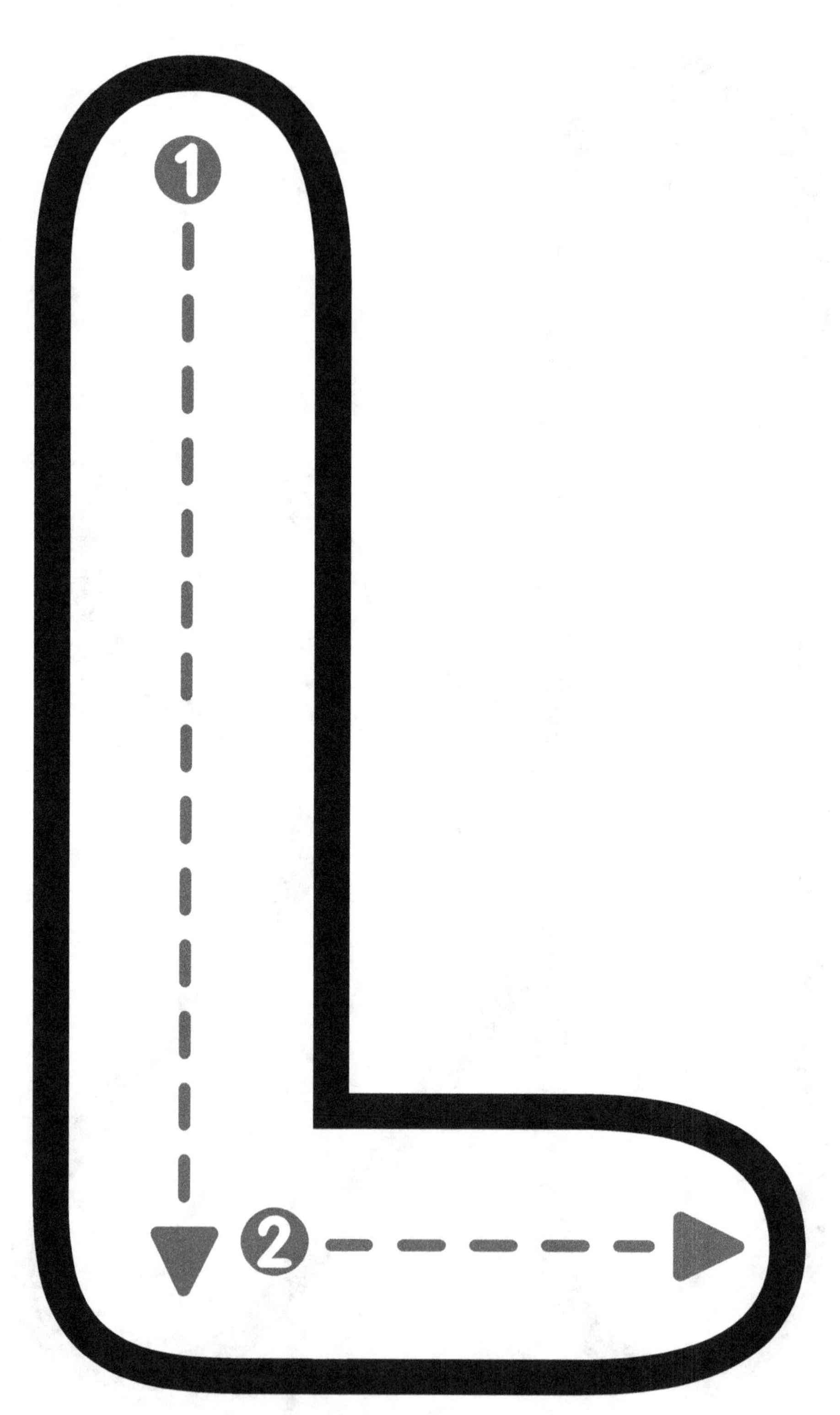

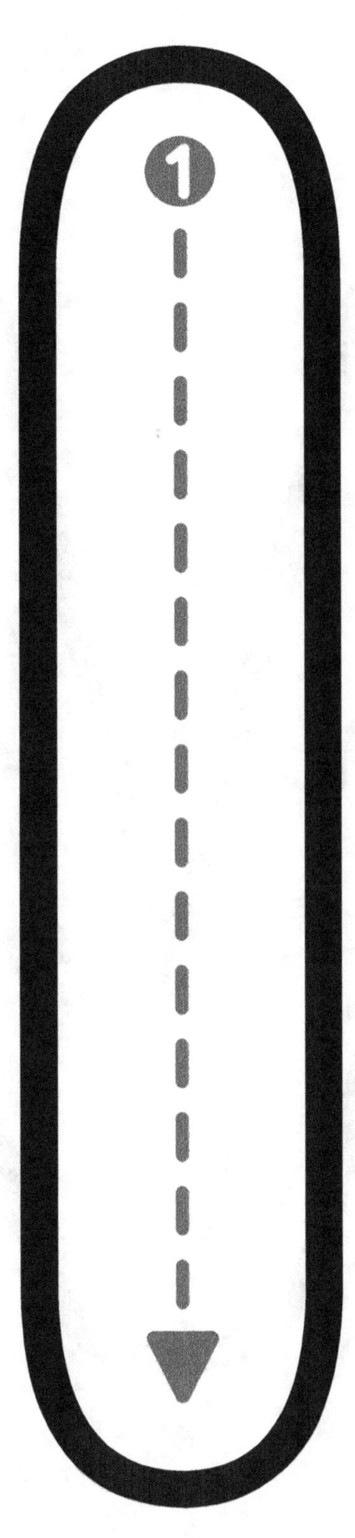

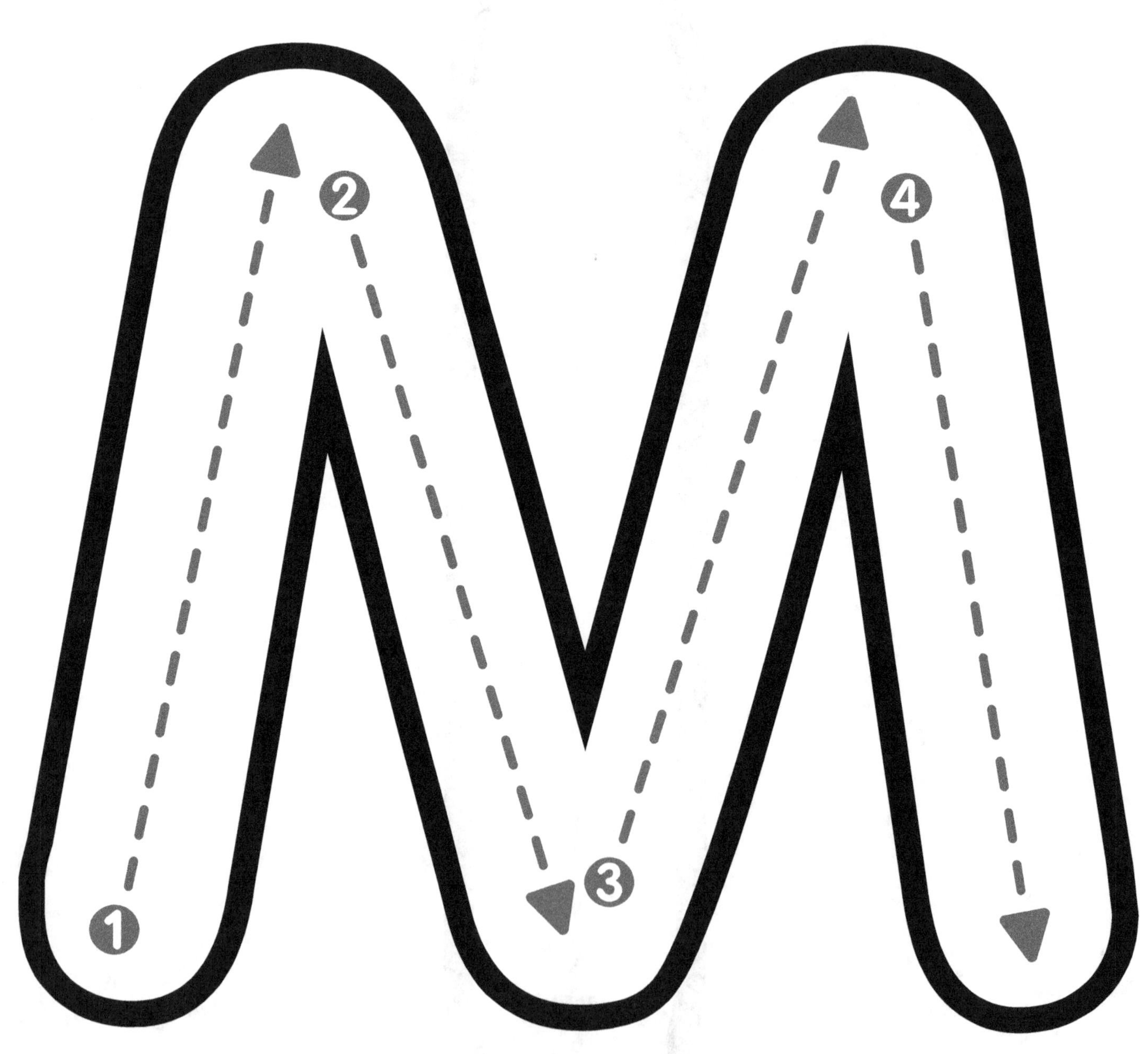

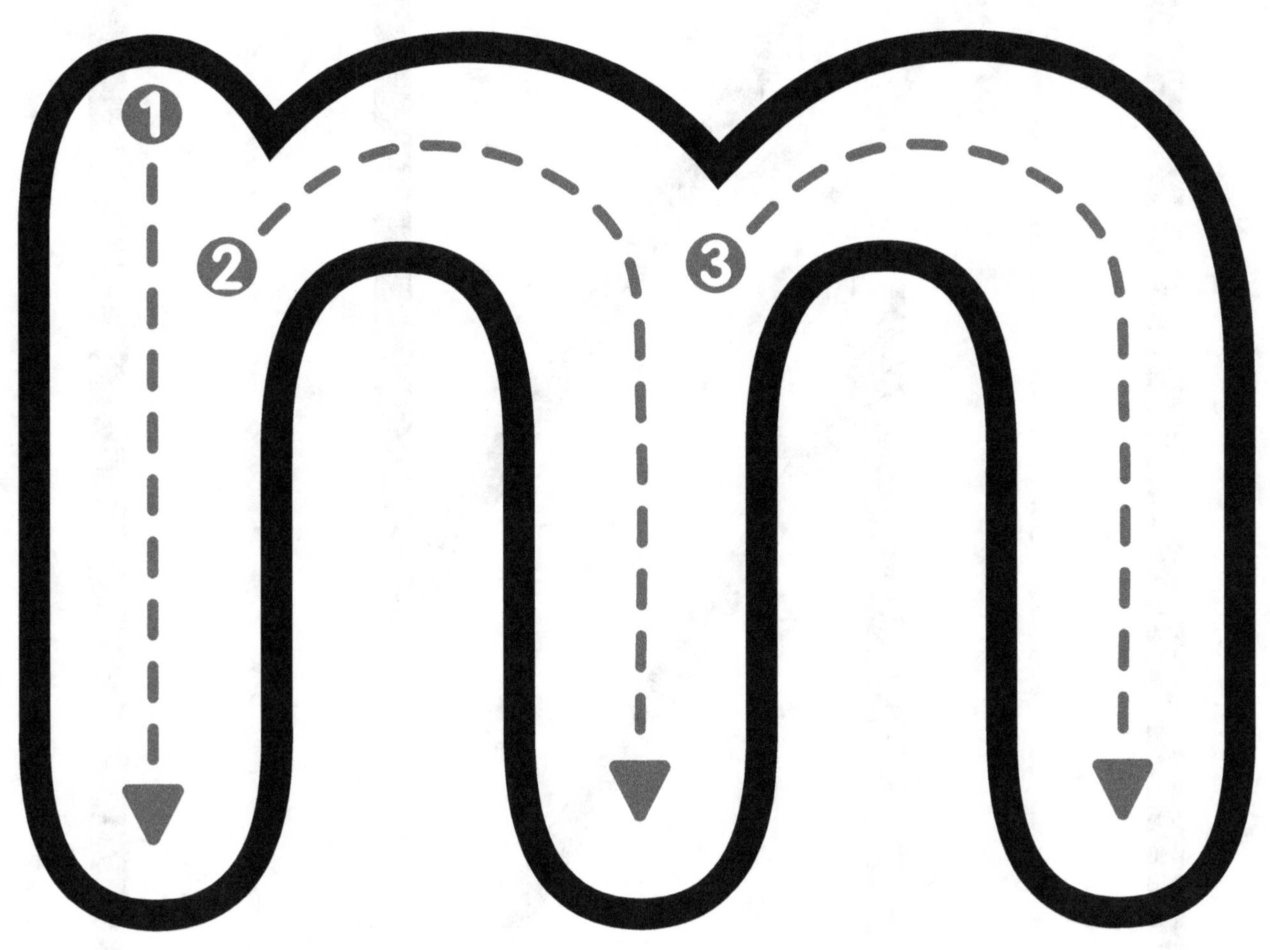

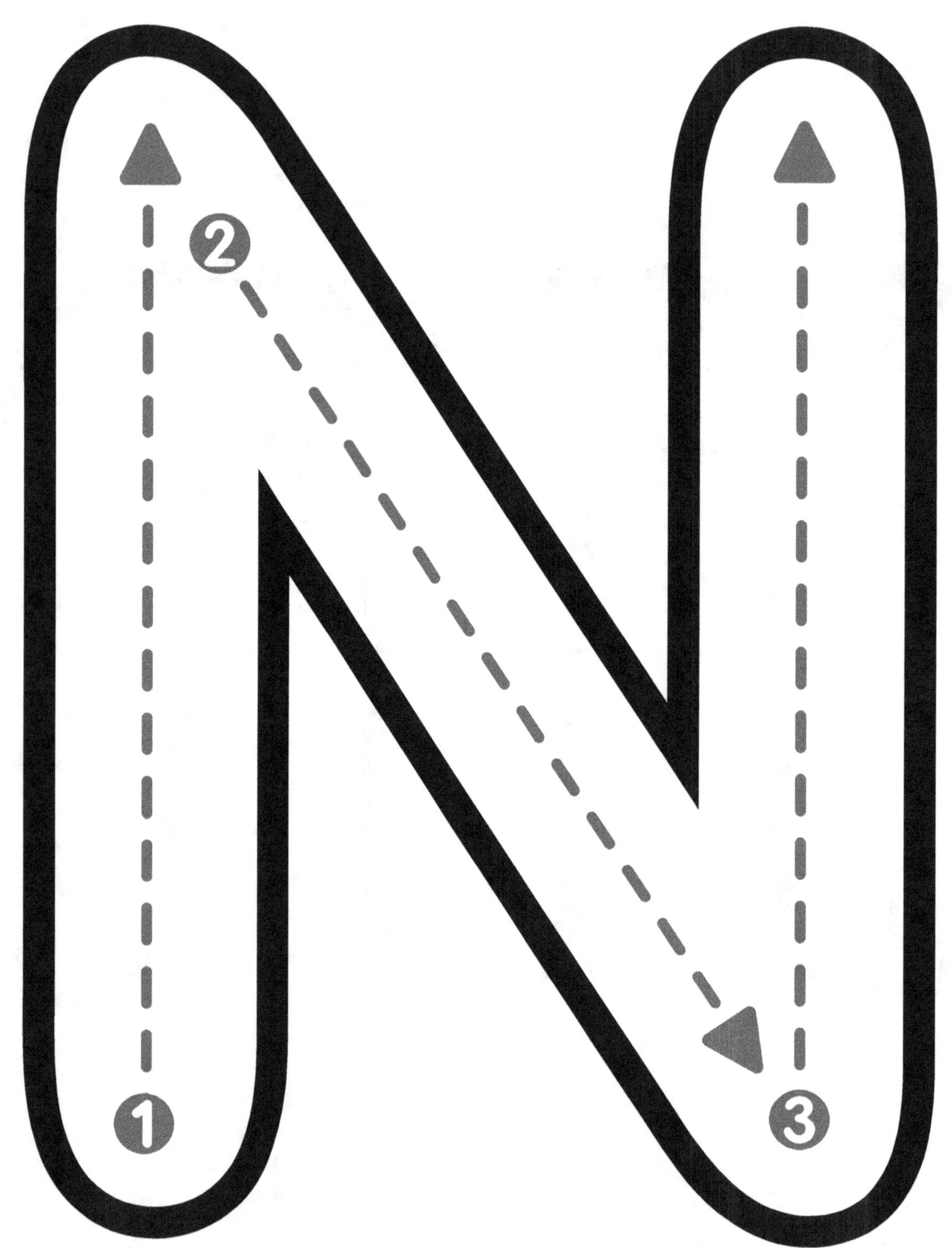

1
2
3

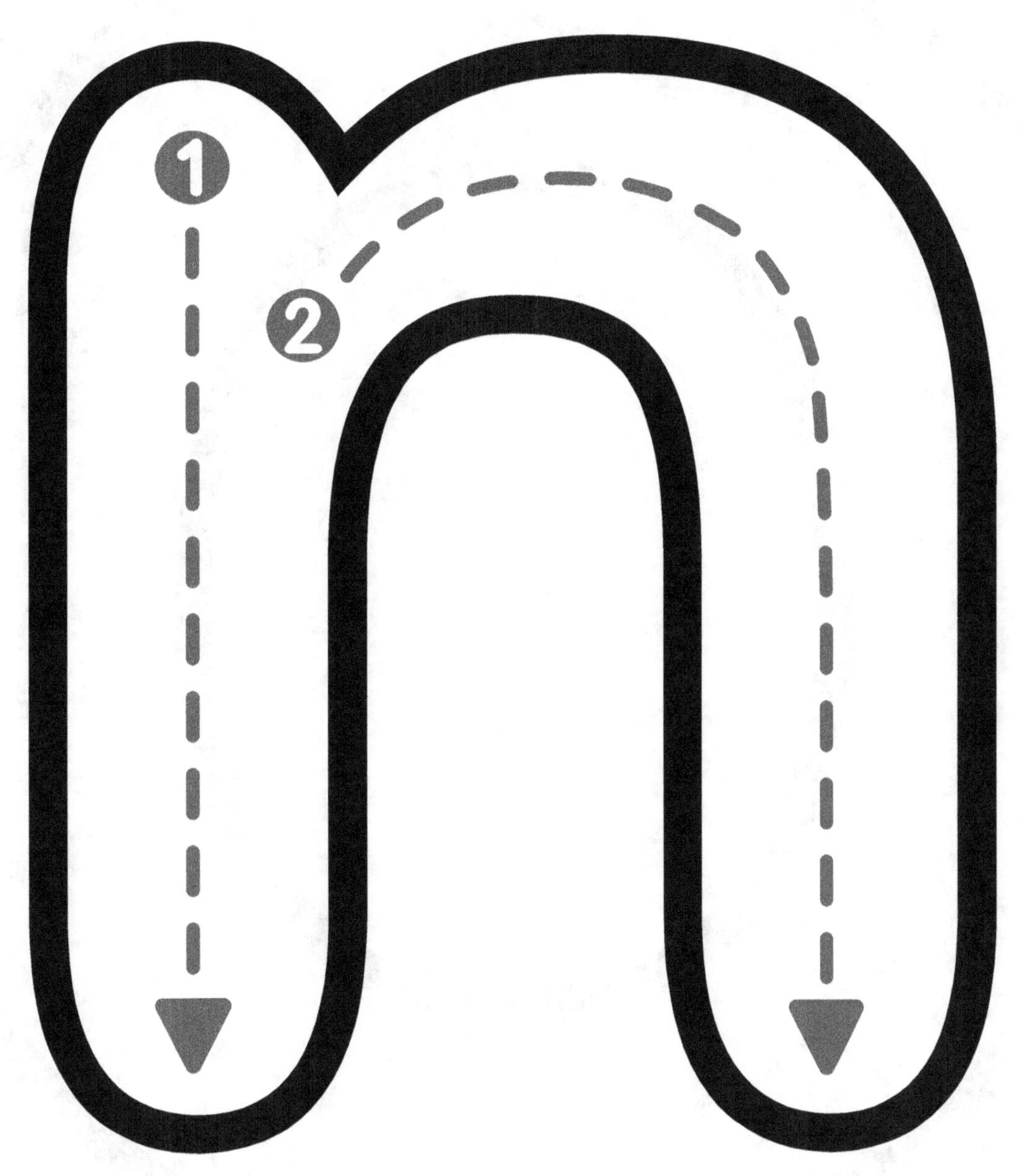

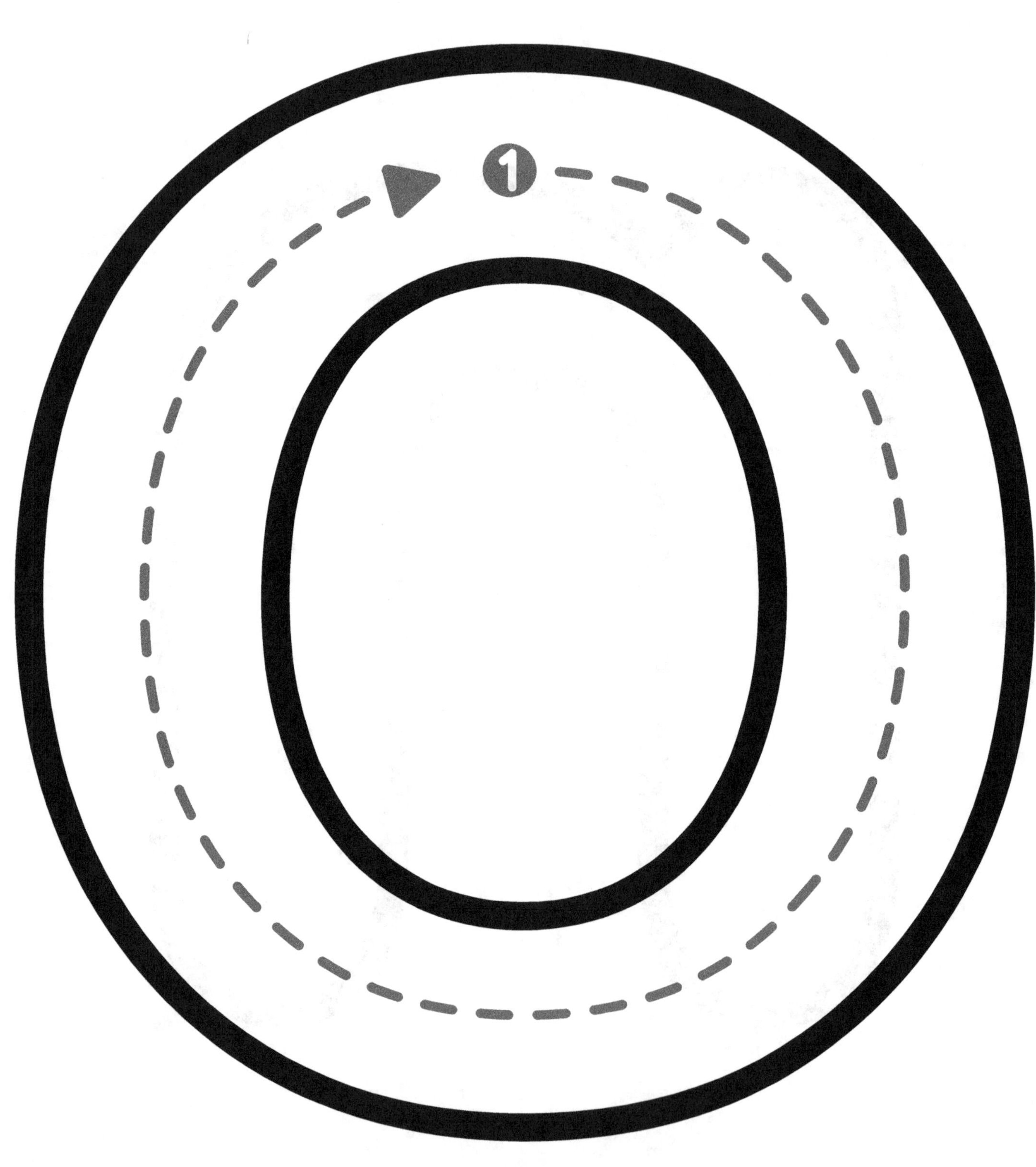
1

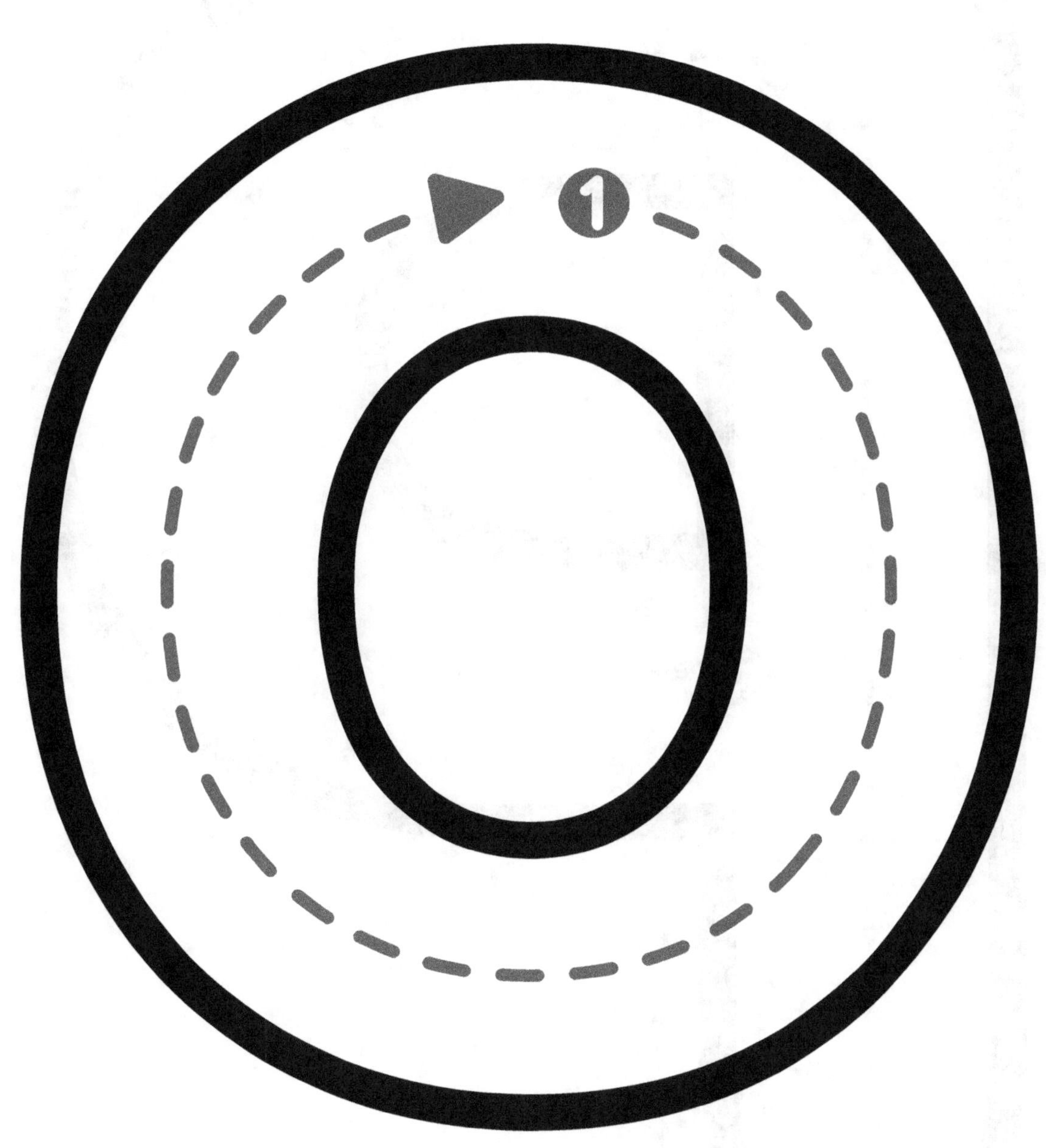

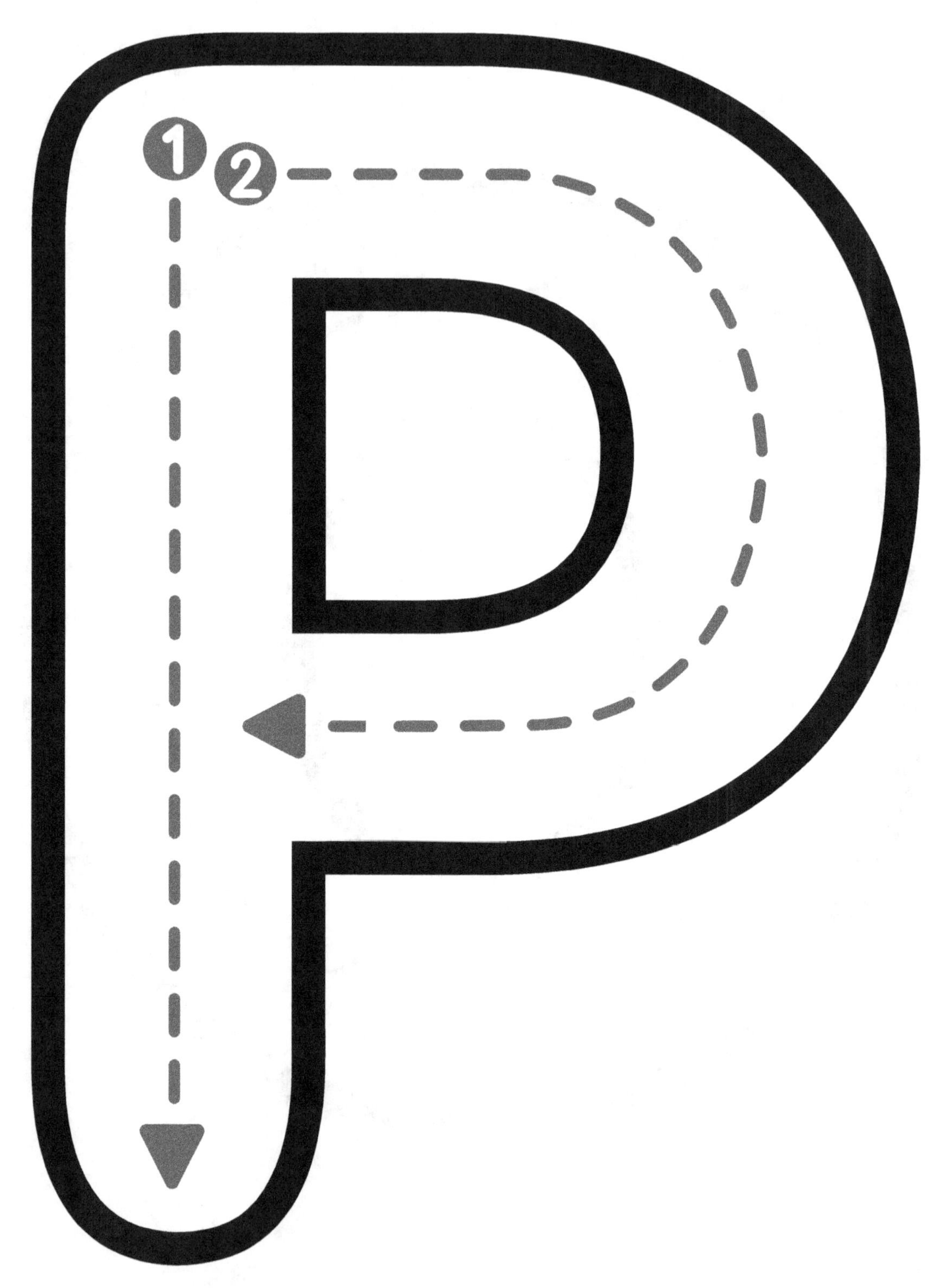

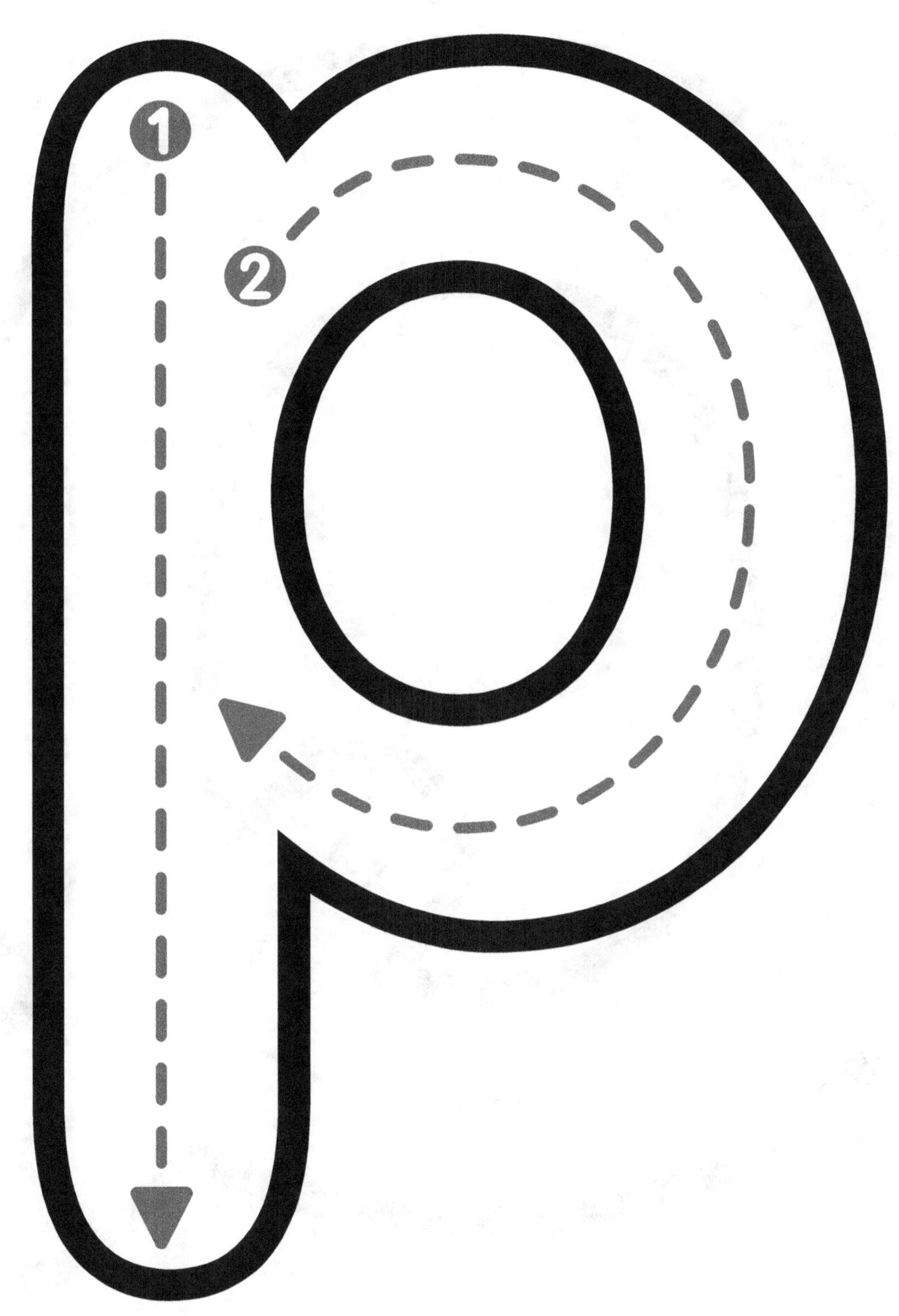

1
2

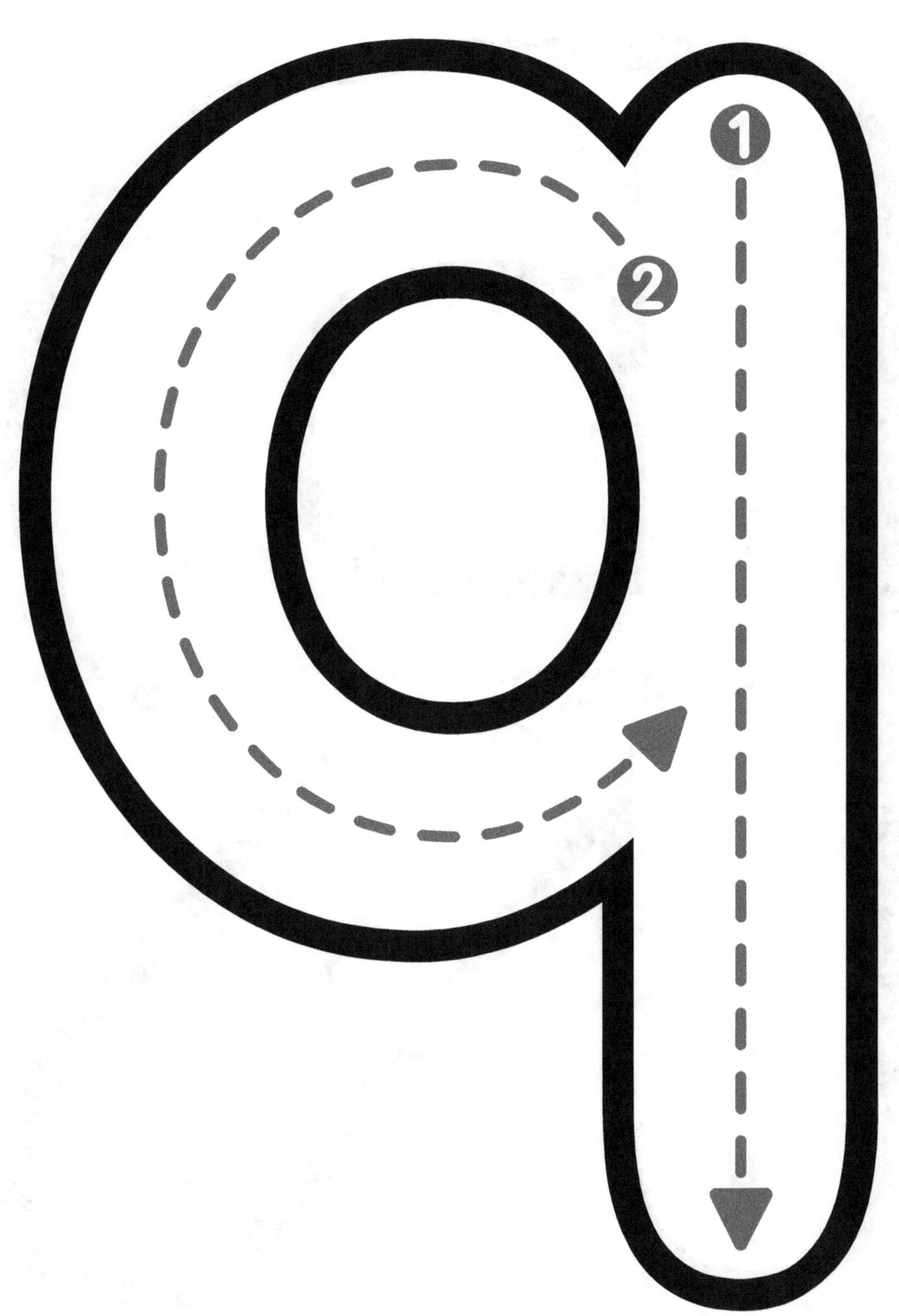

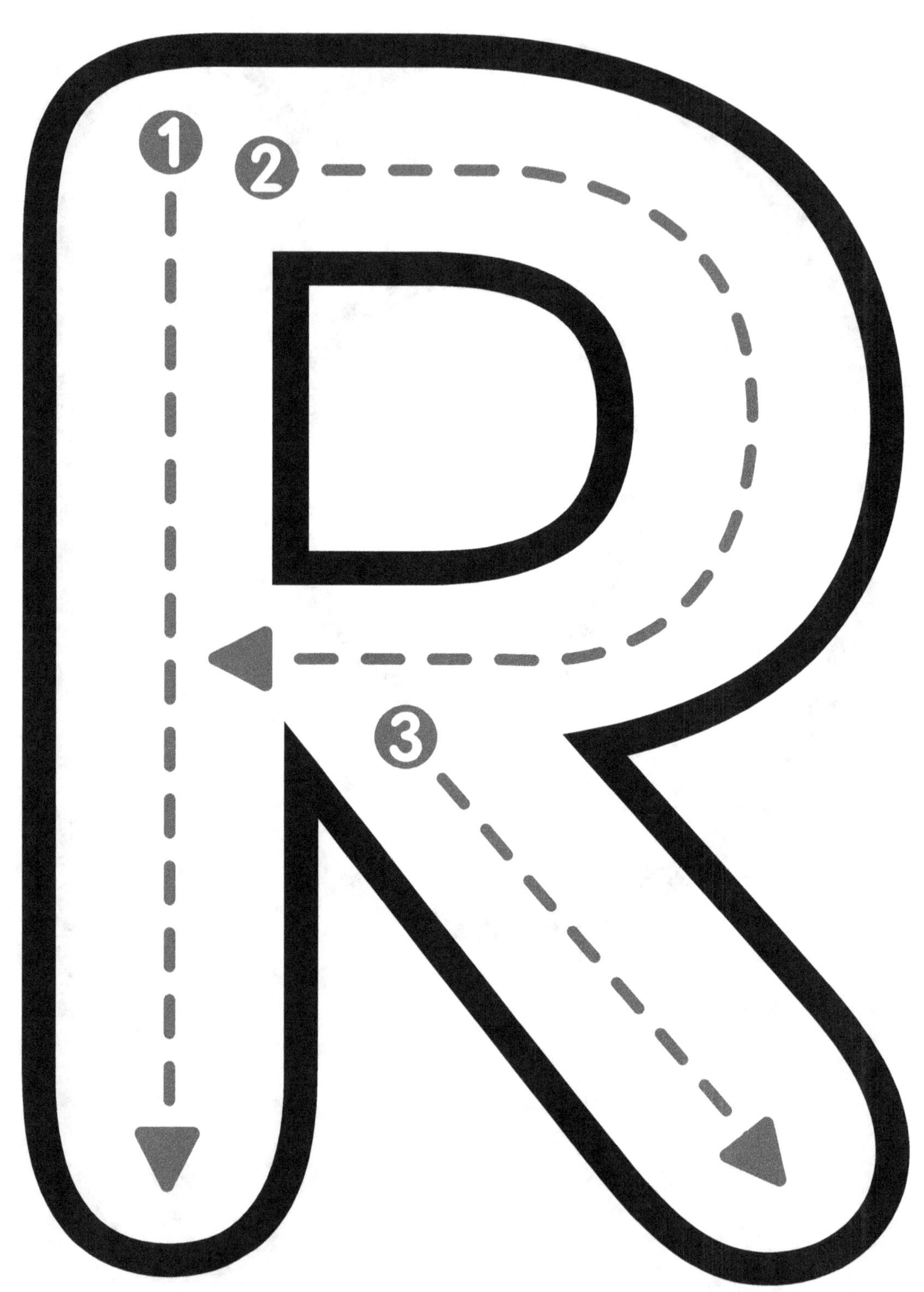

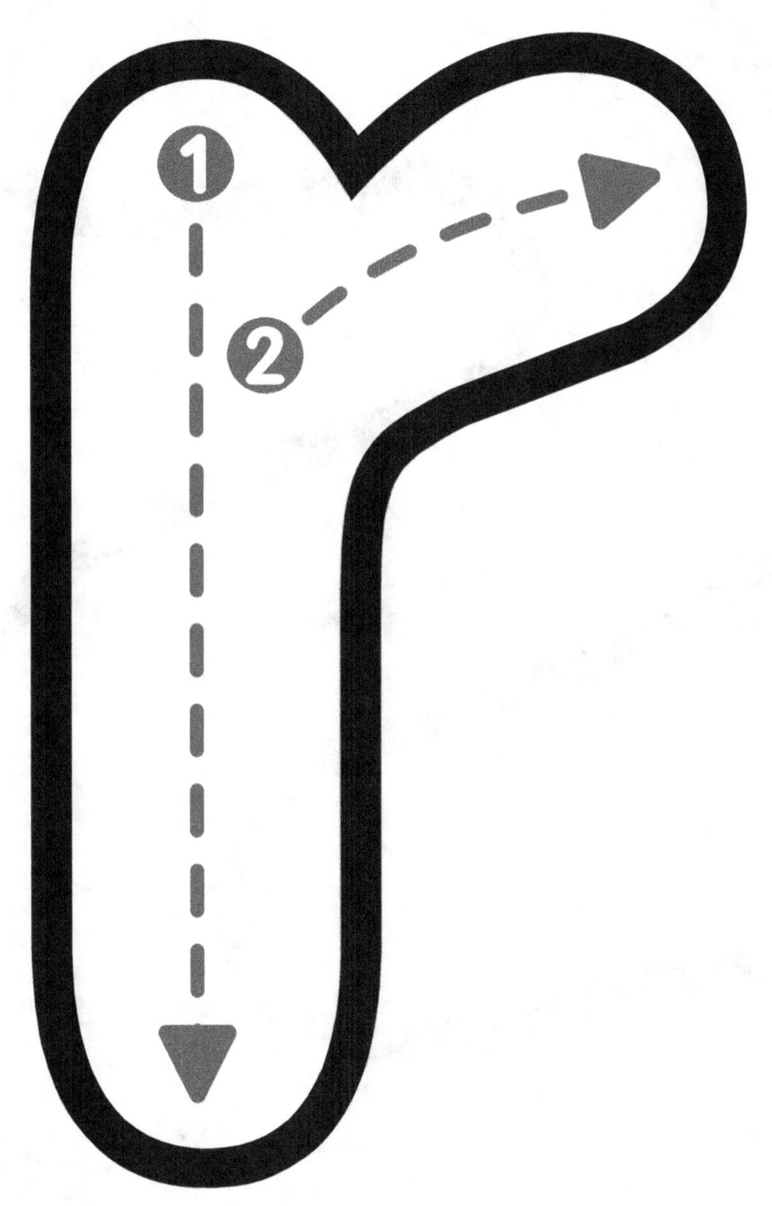

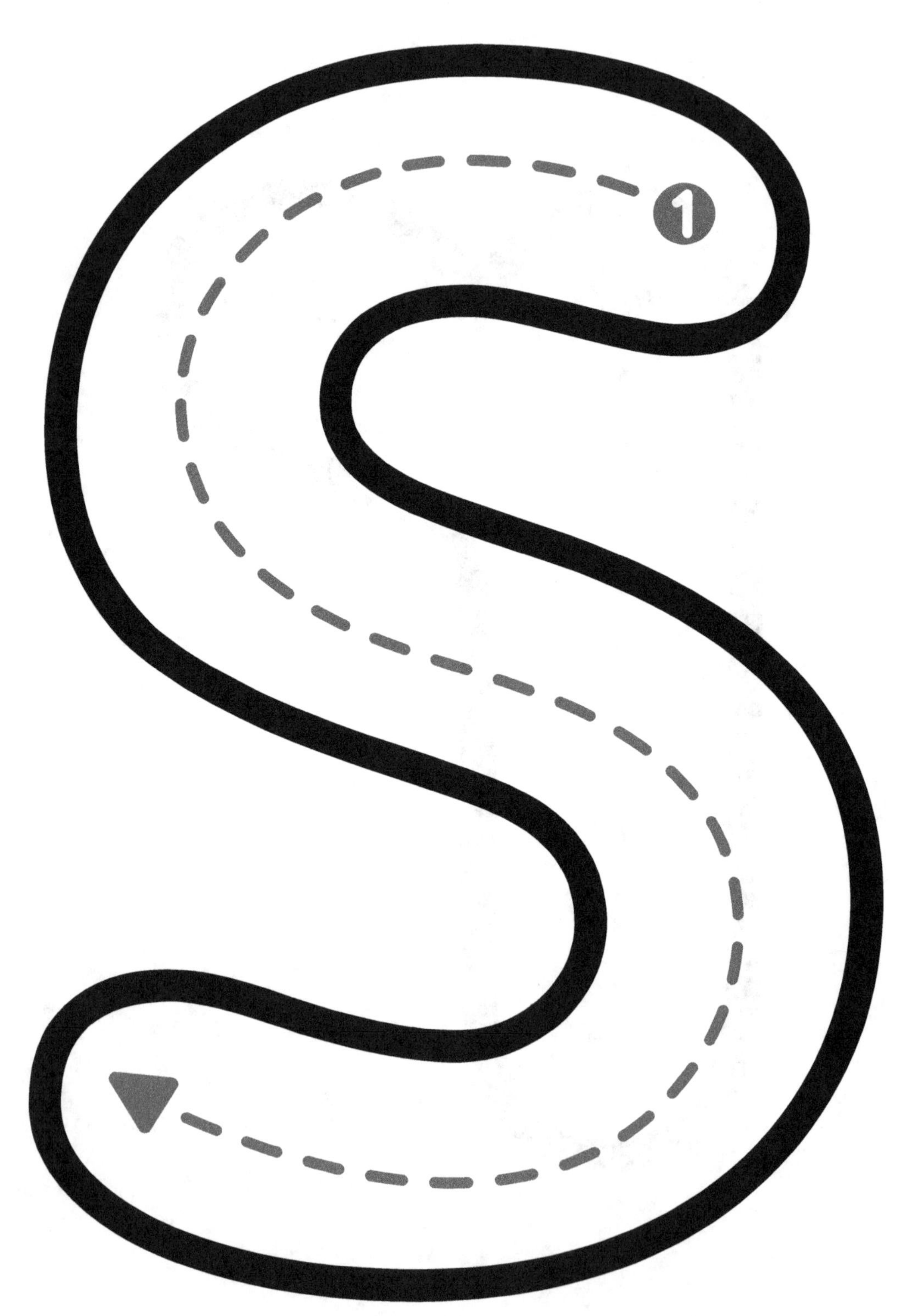

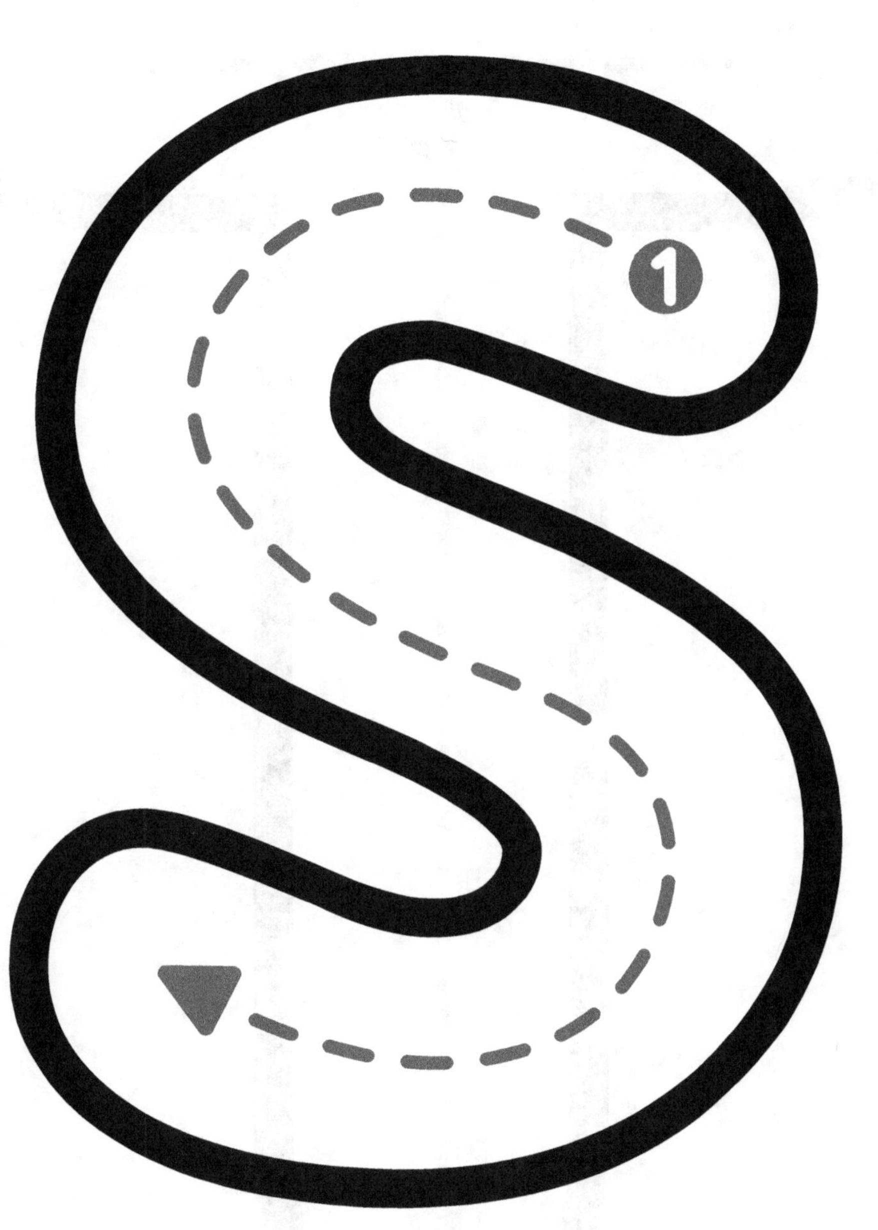
1

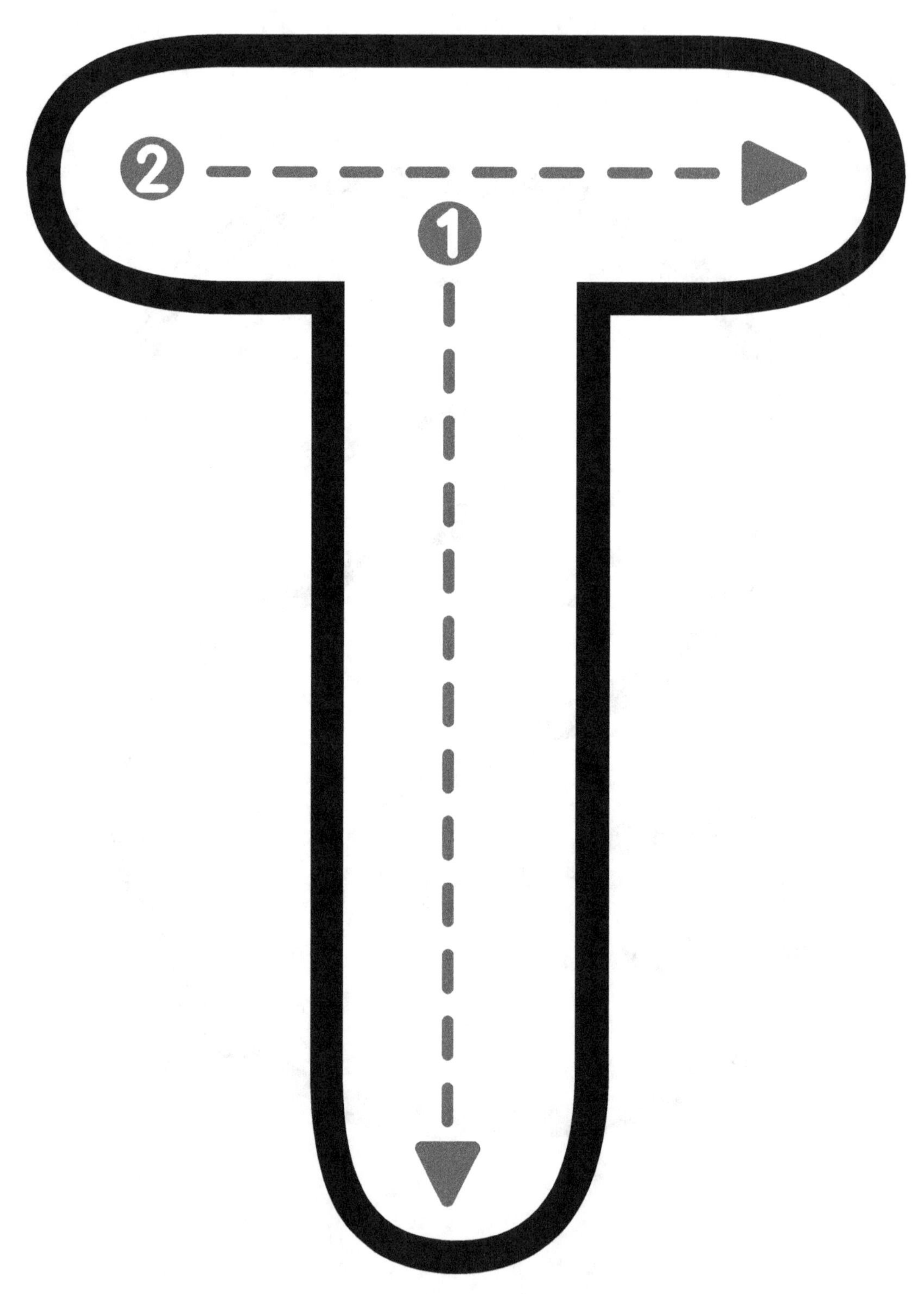

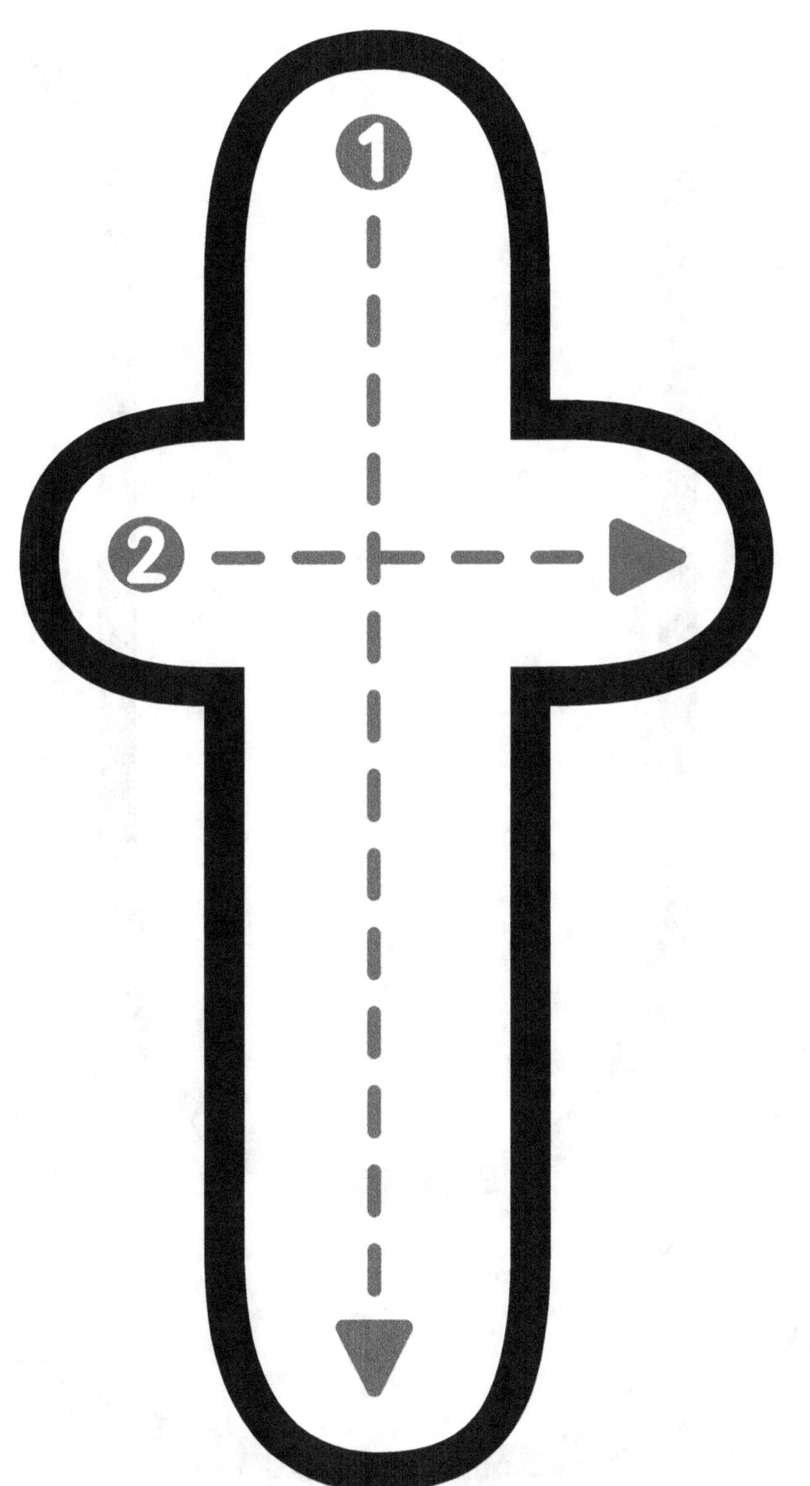

1
2

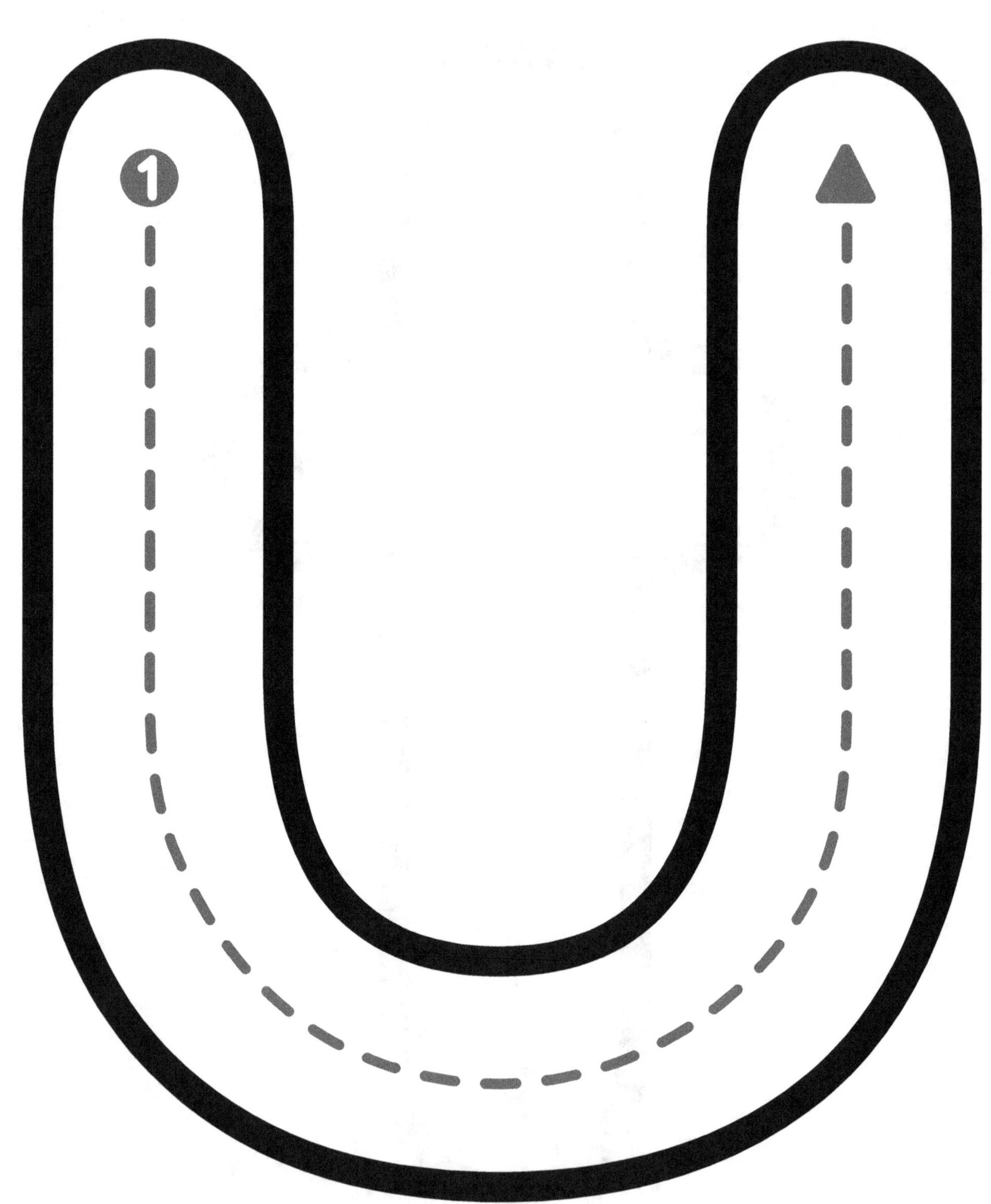

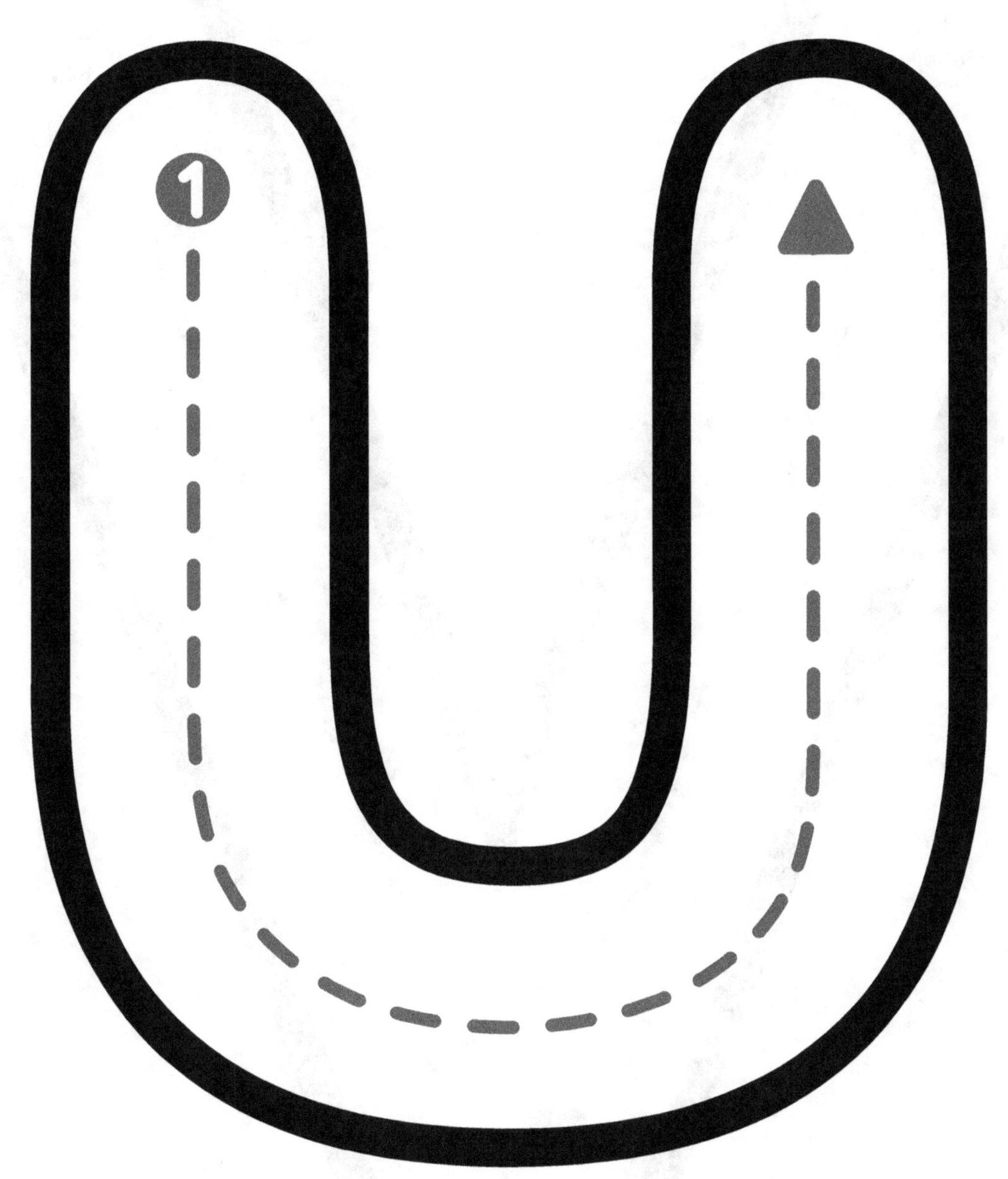

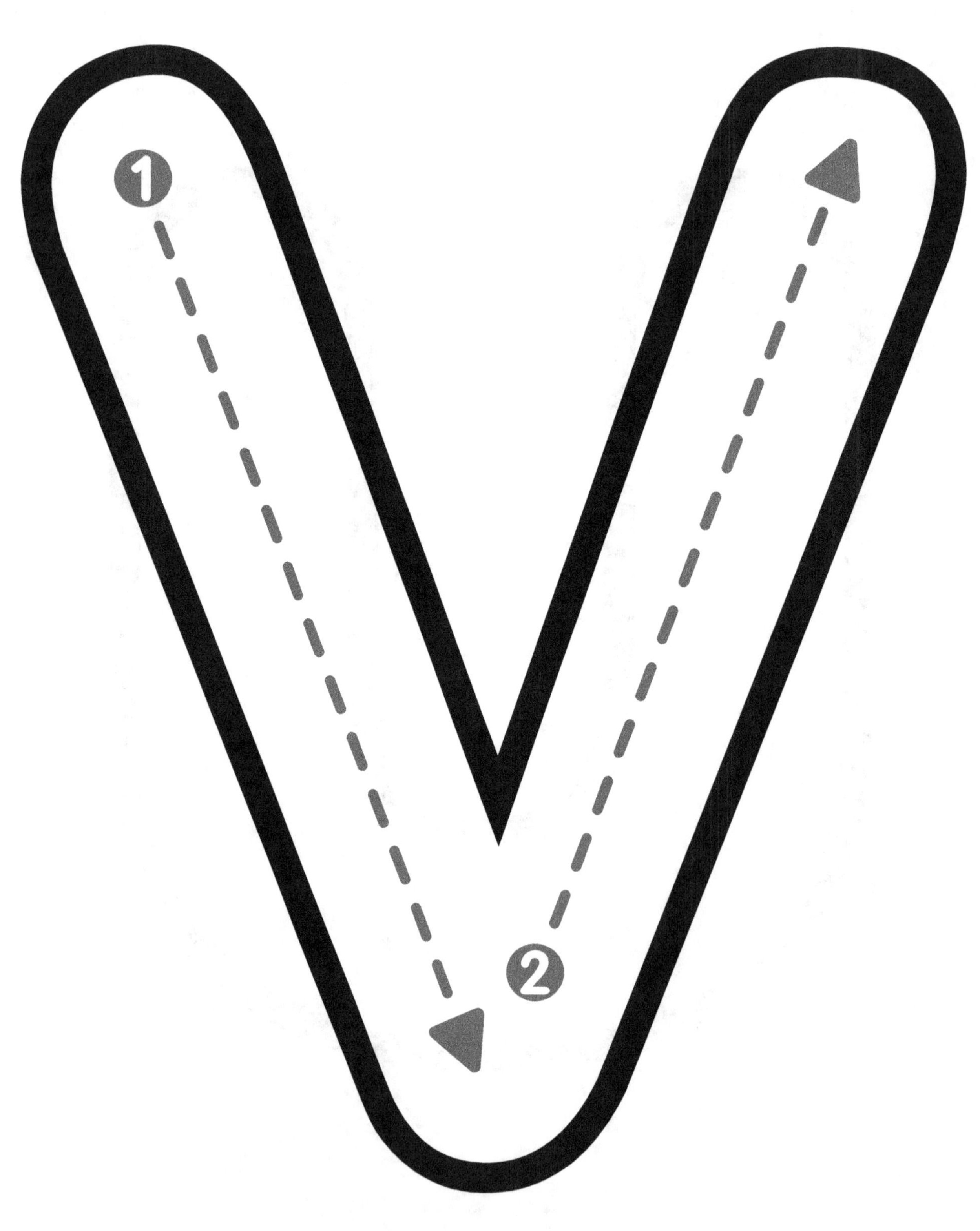

1
2

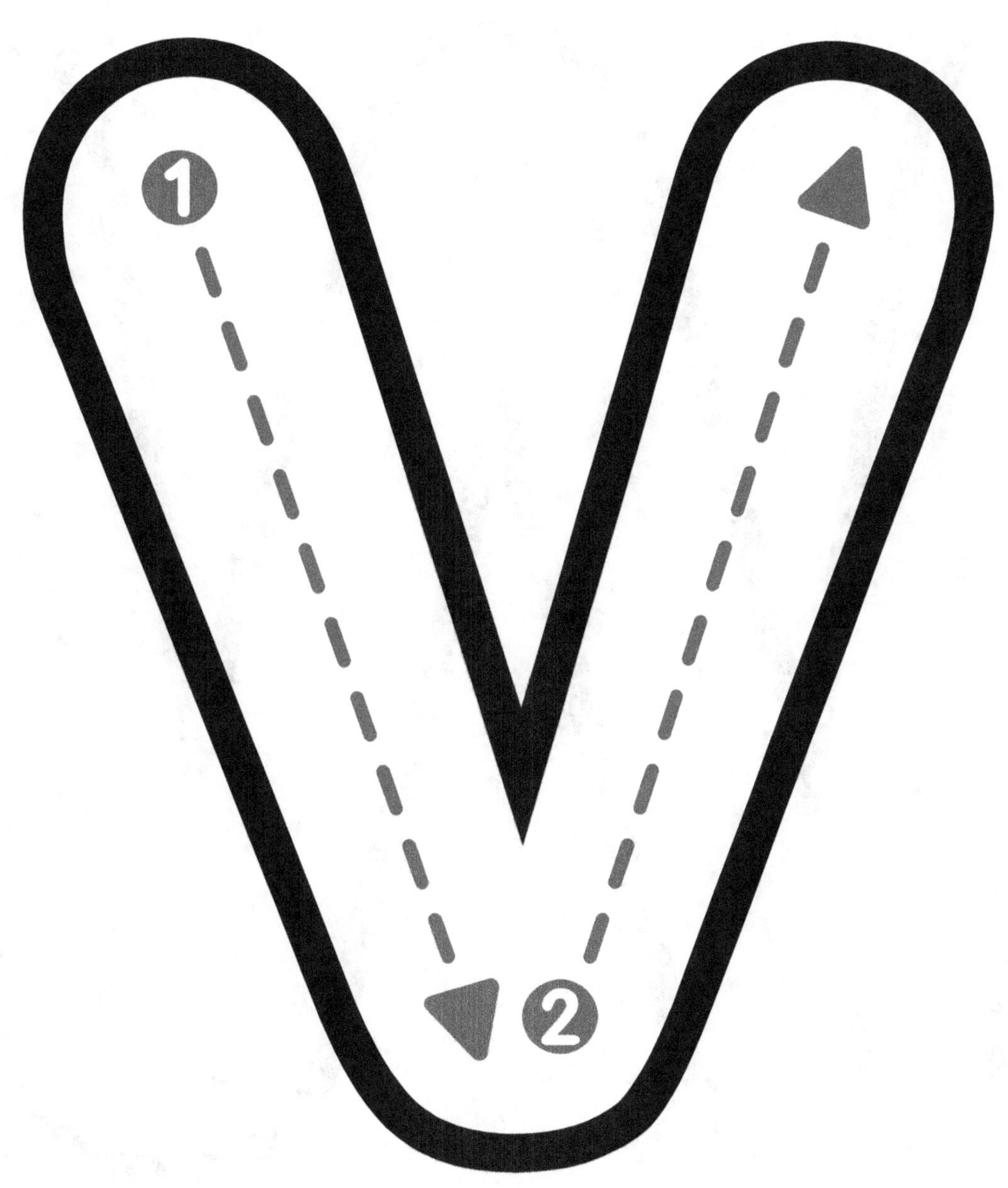

1
2

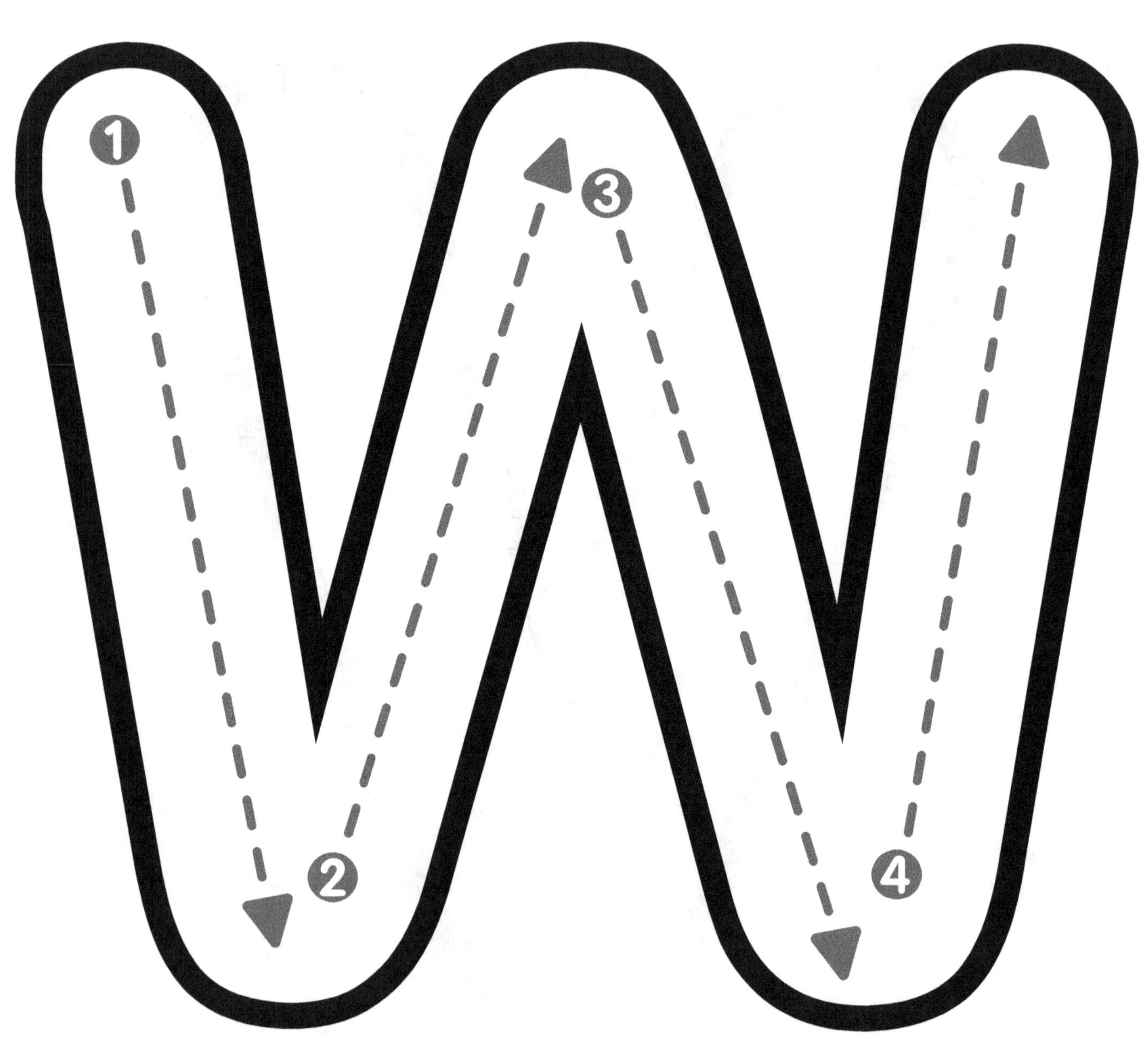

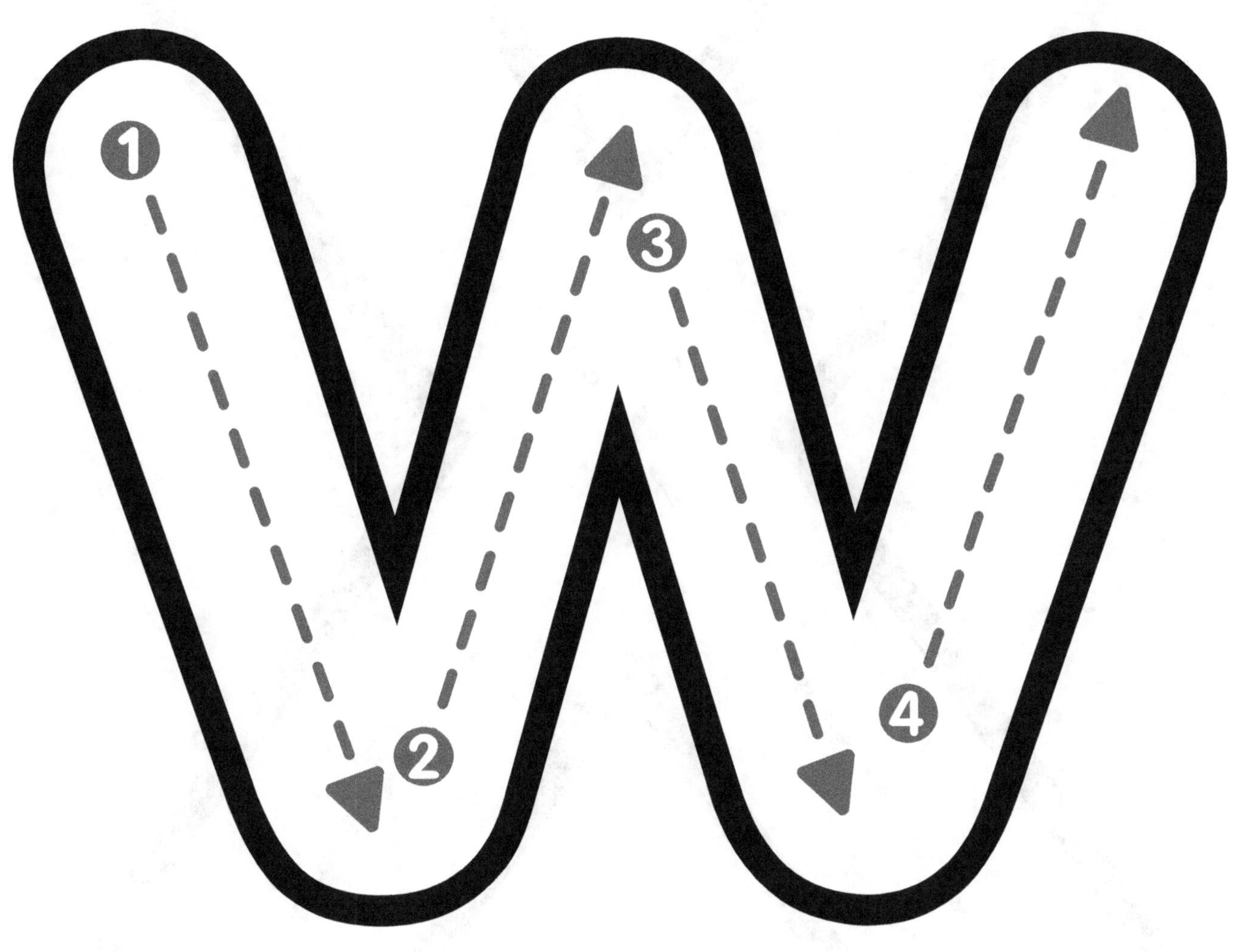

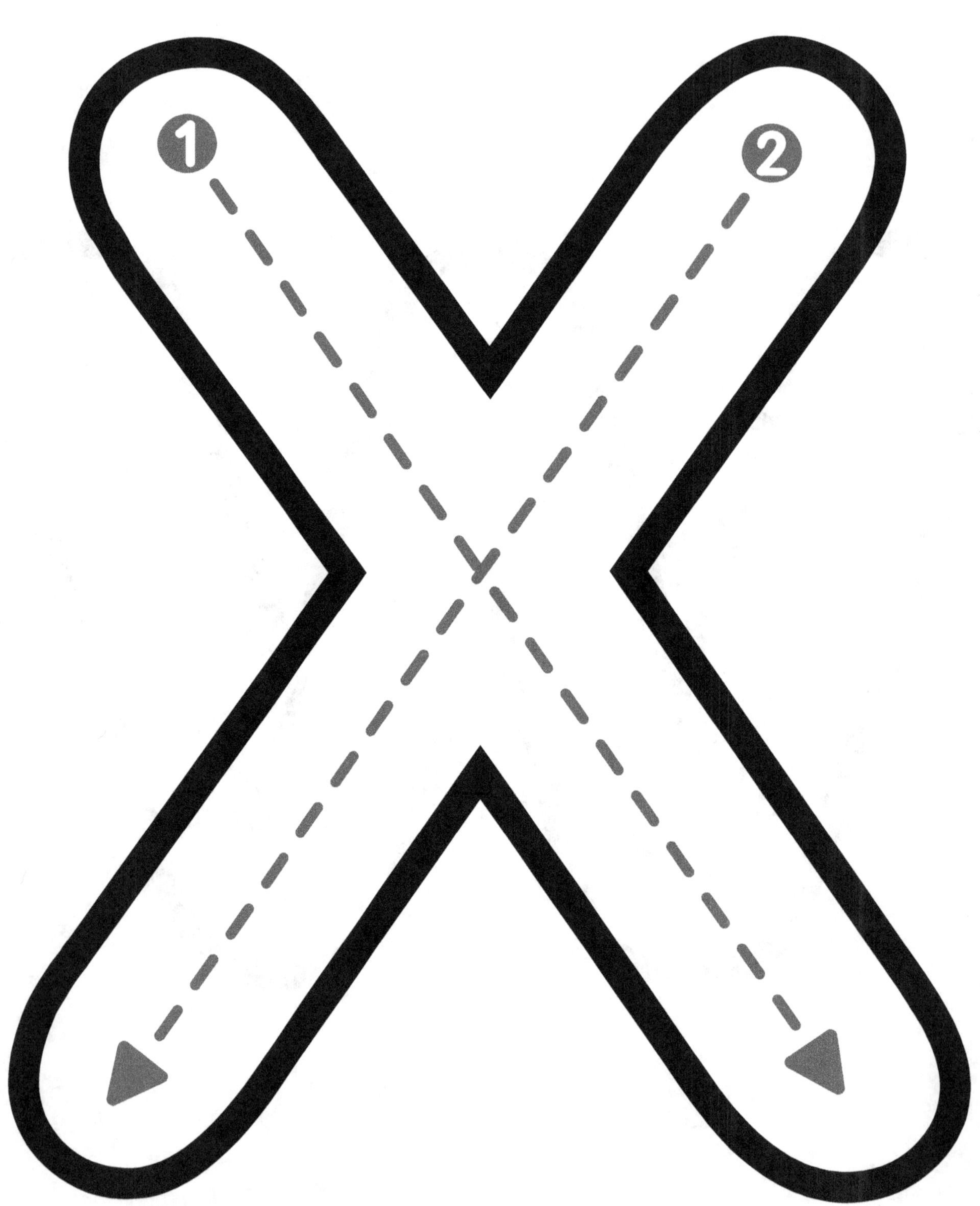
1
2

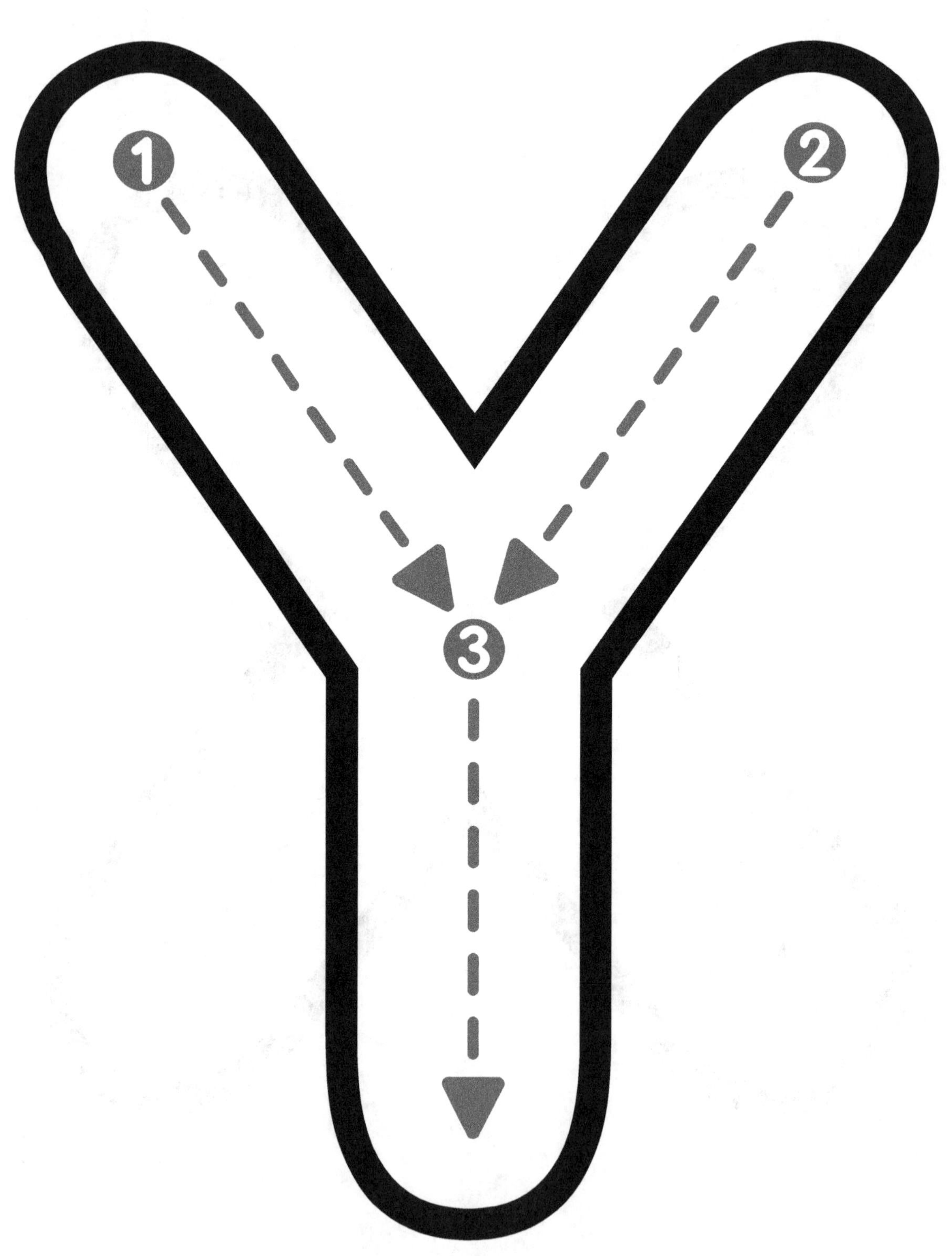

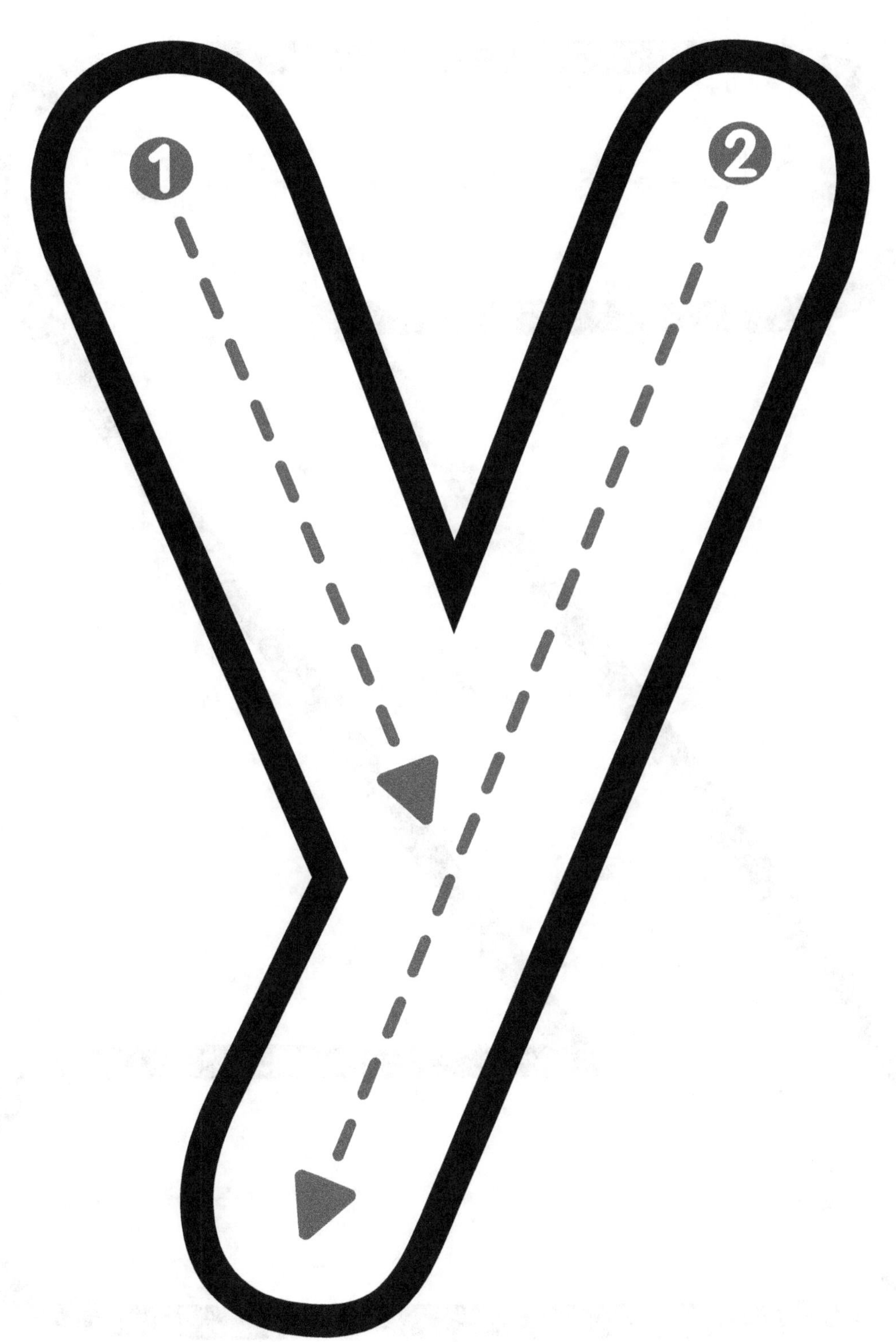

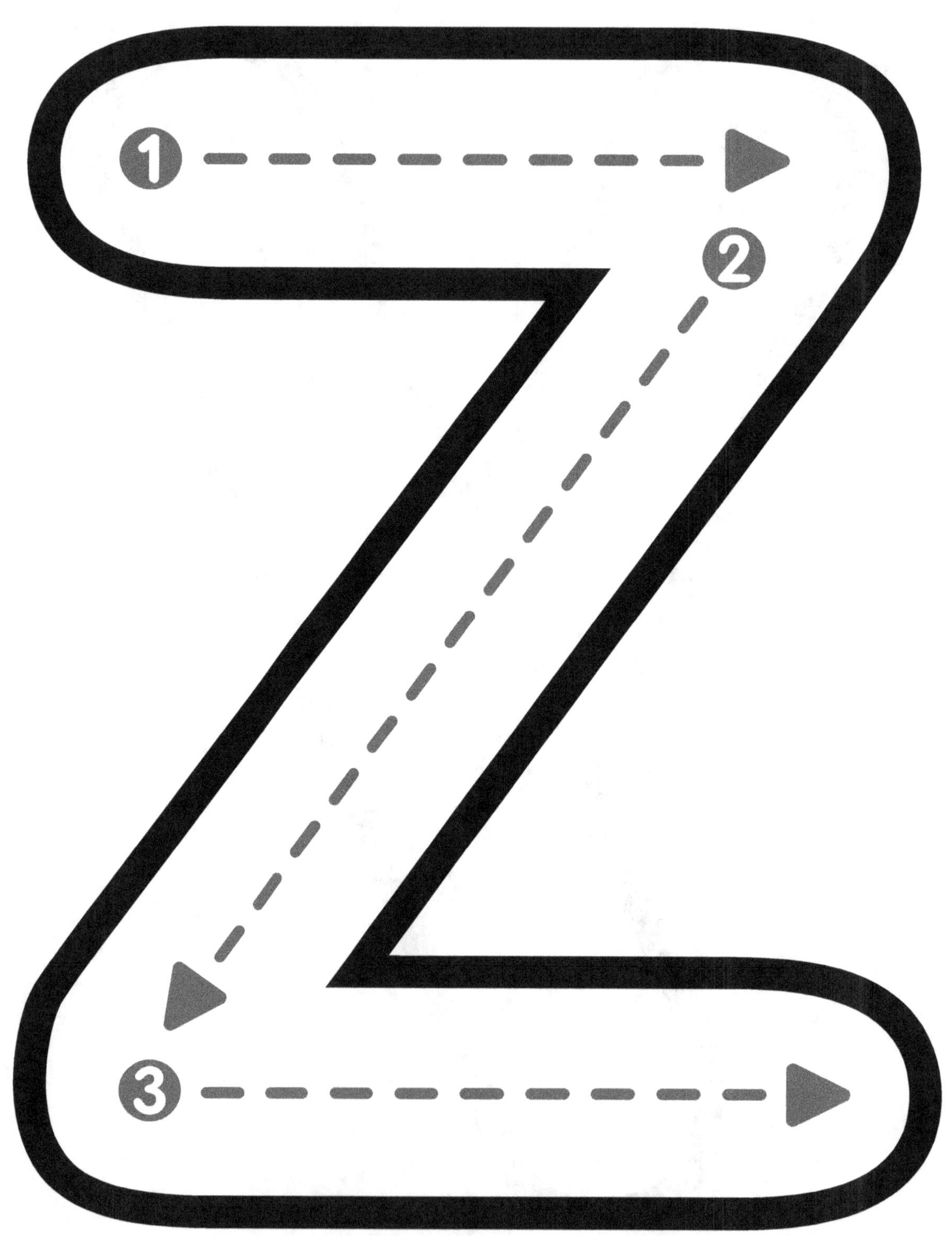

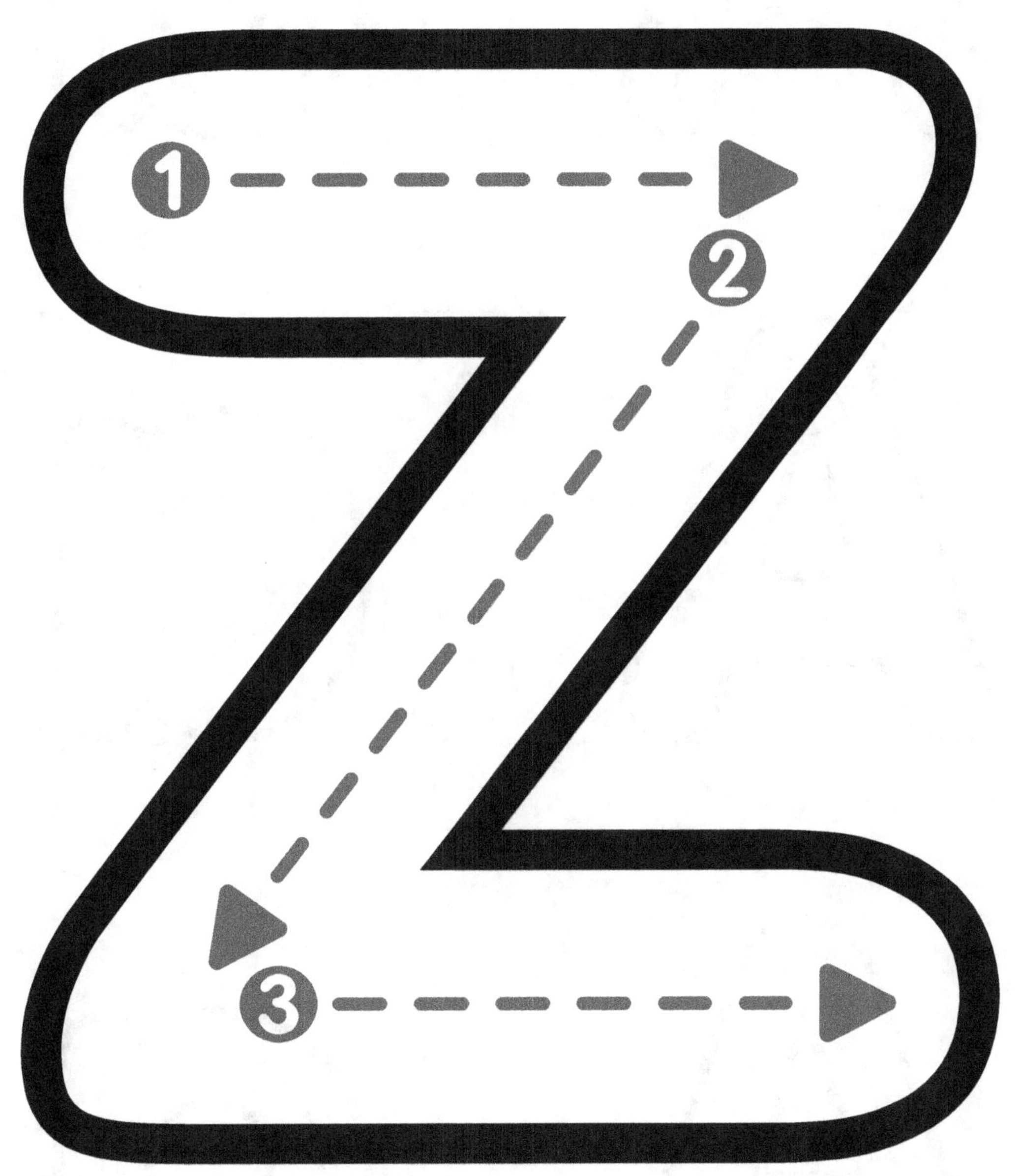
1
2
3

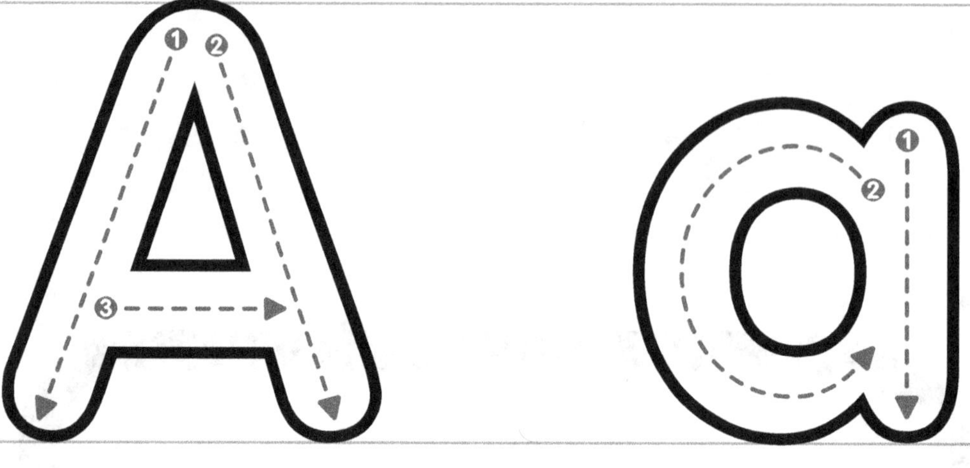

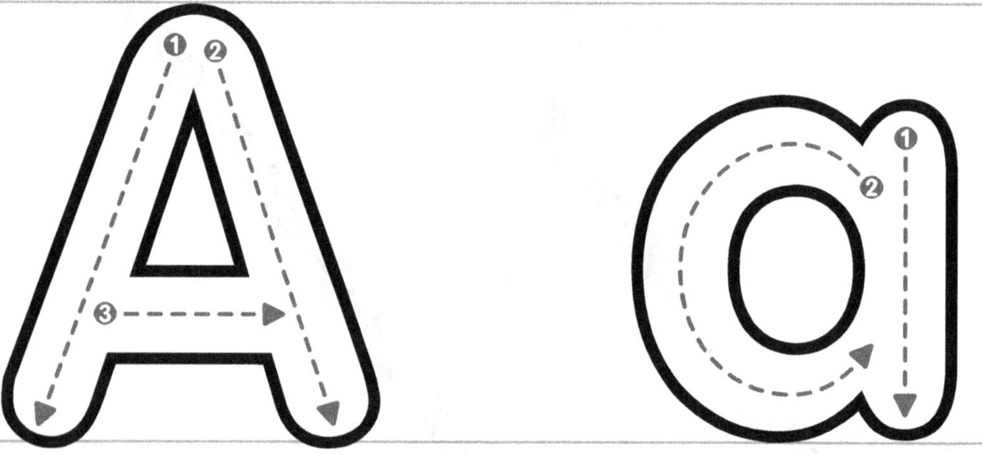

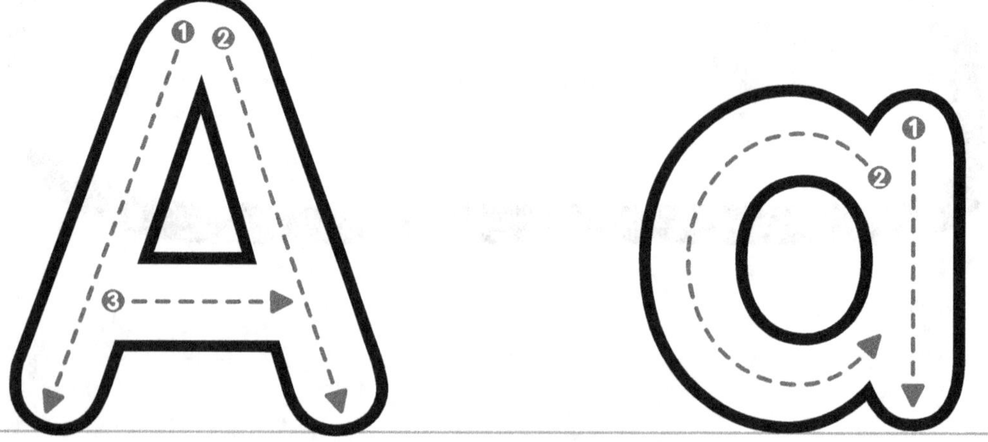

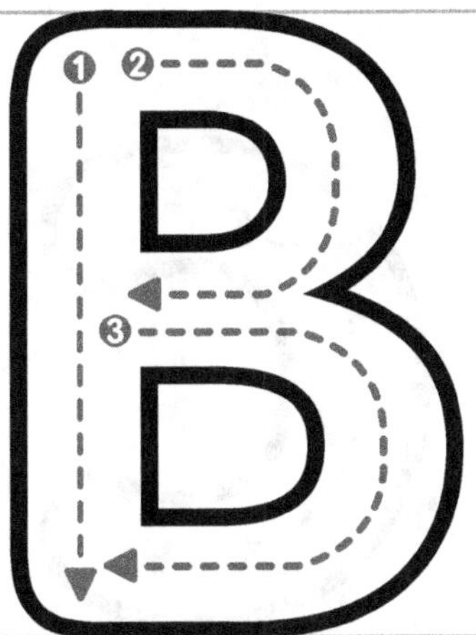

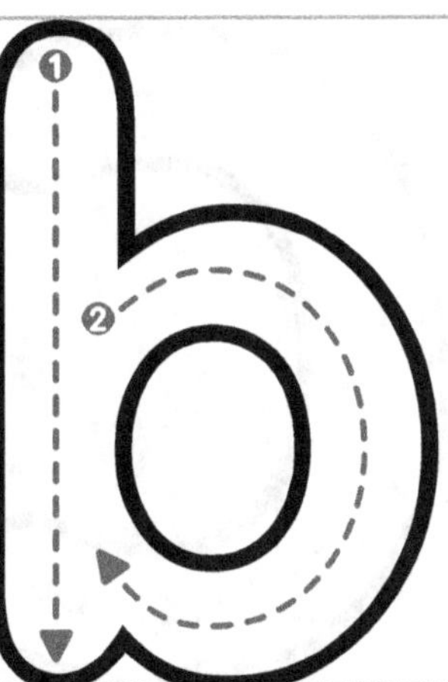
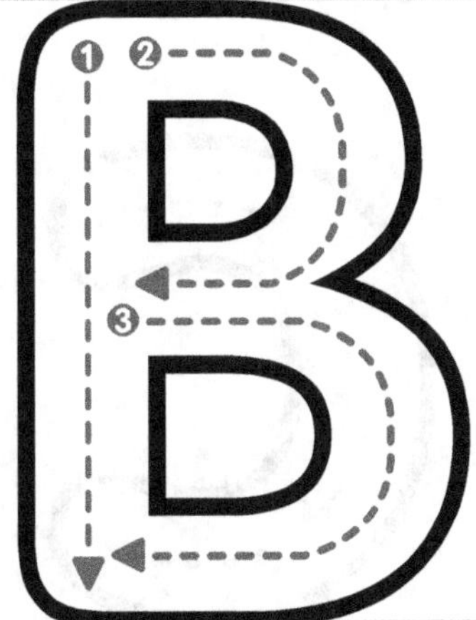
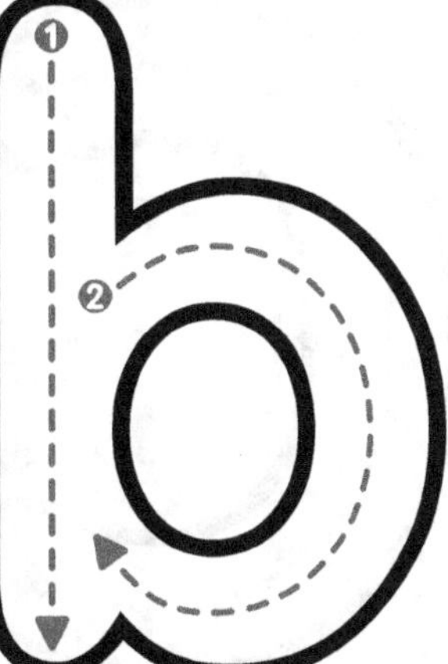

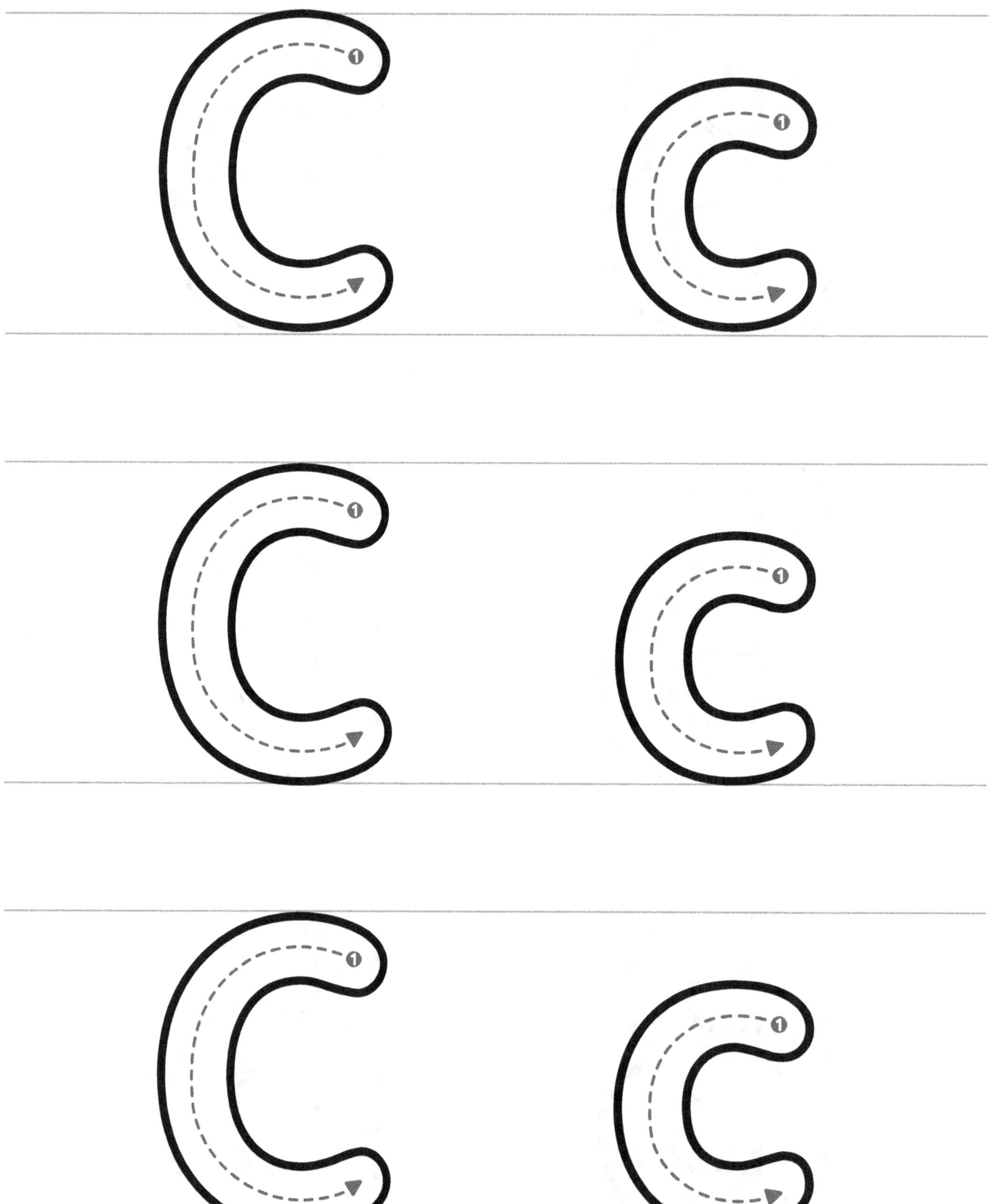

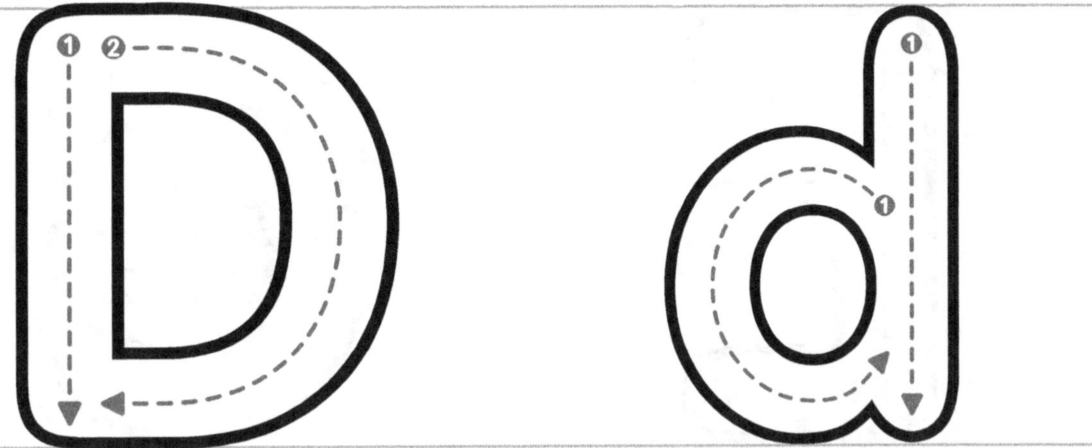

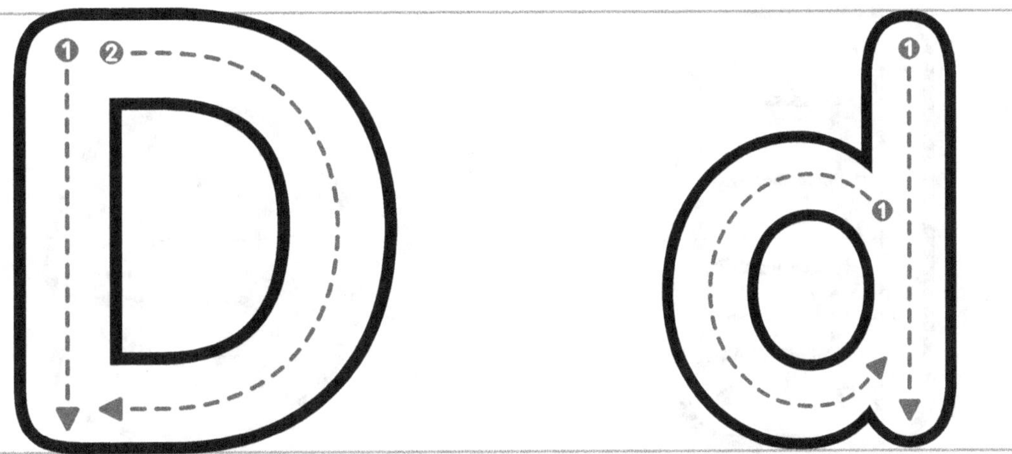

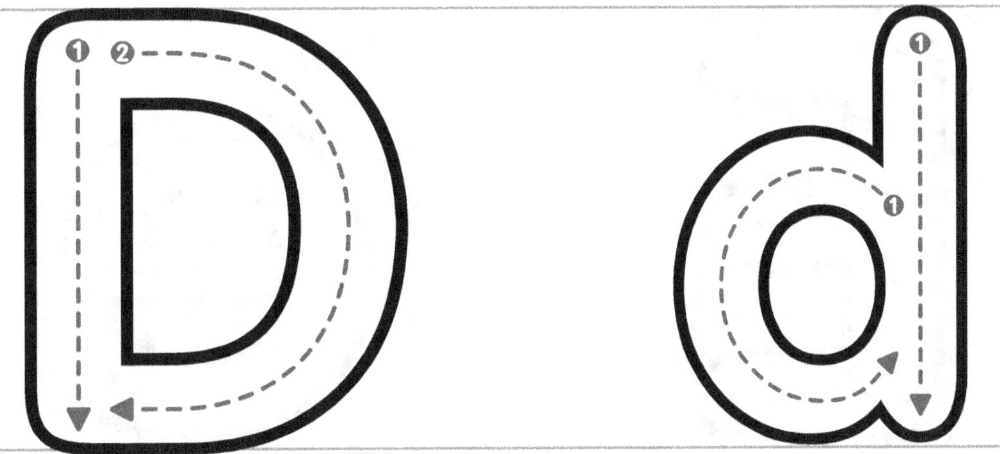

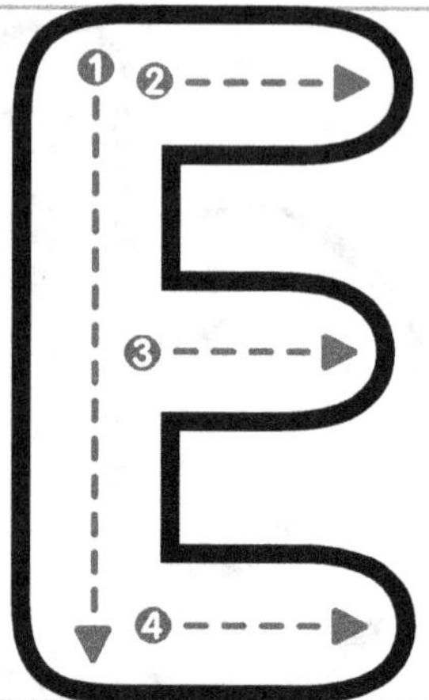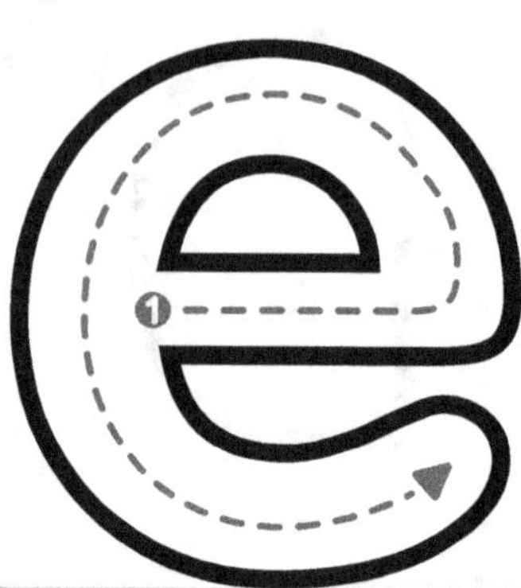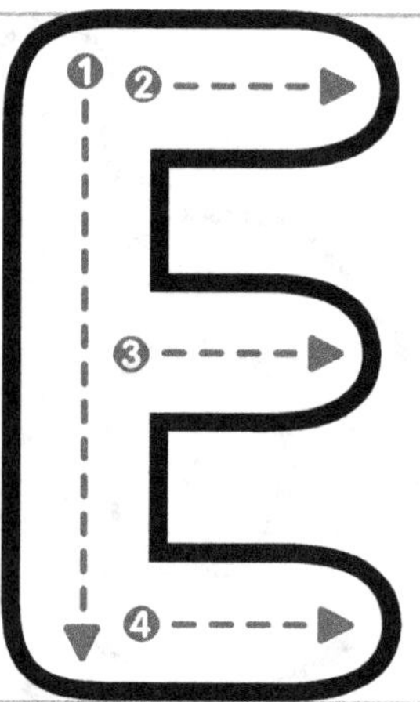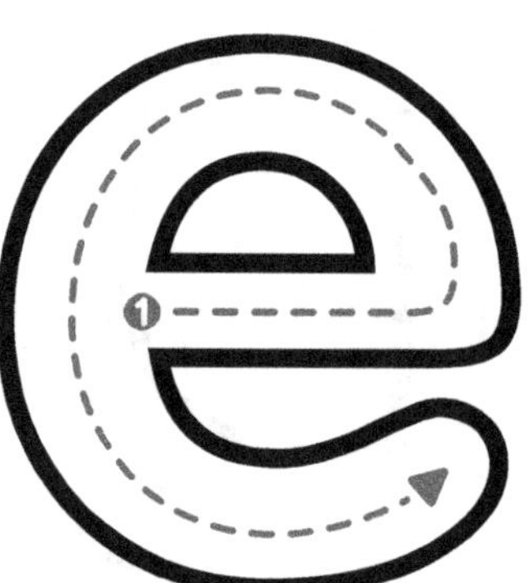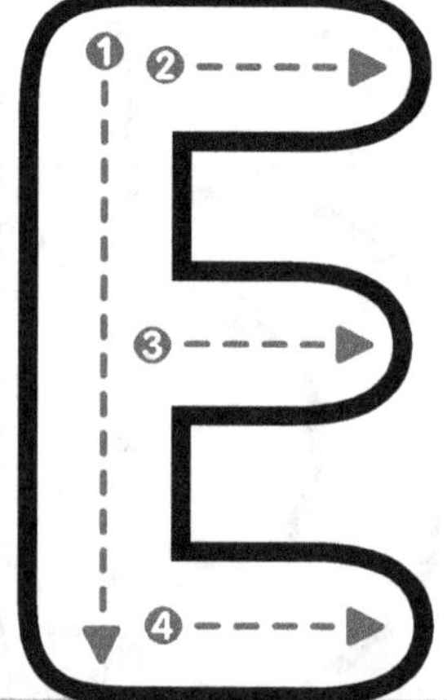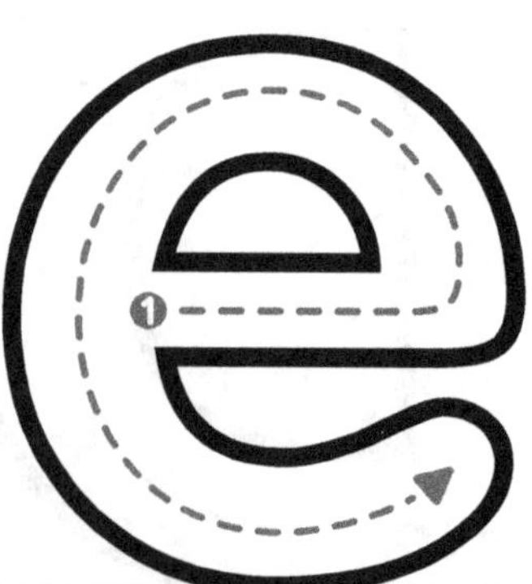

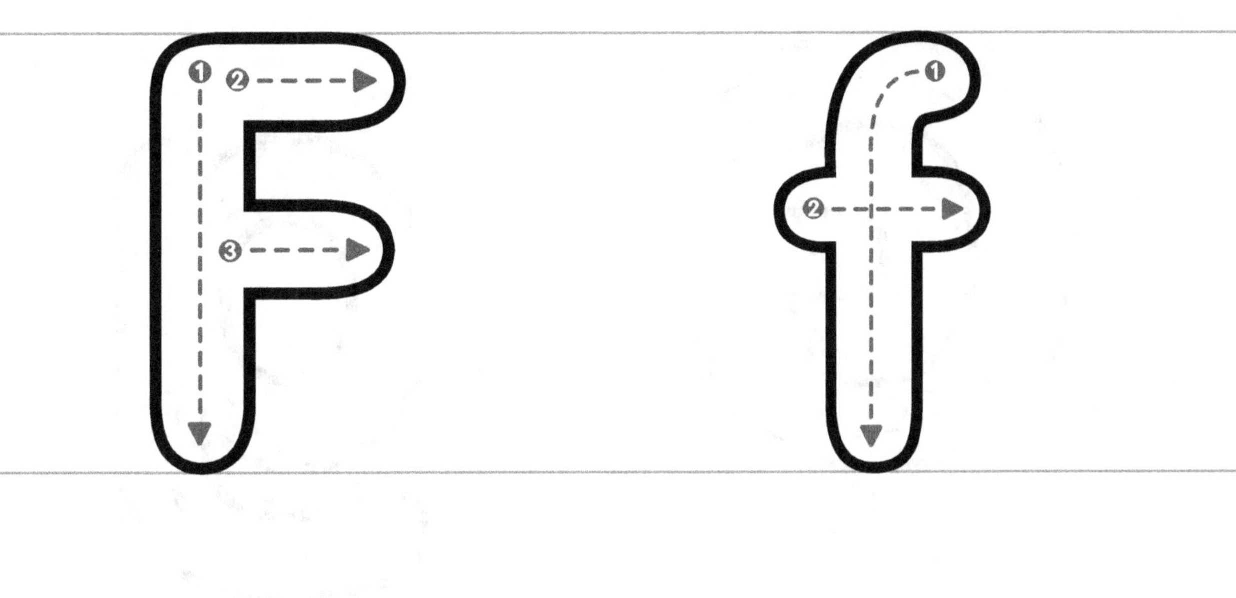

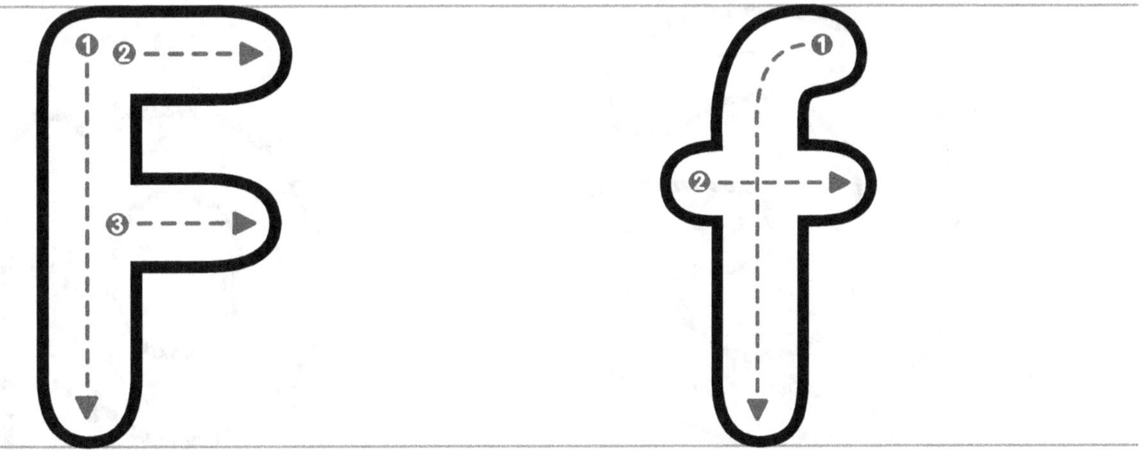

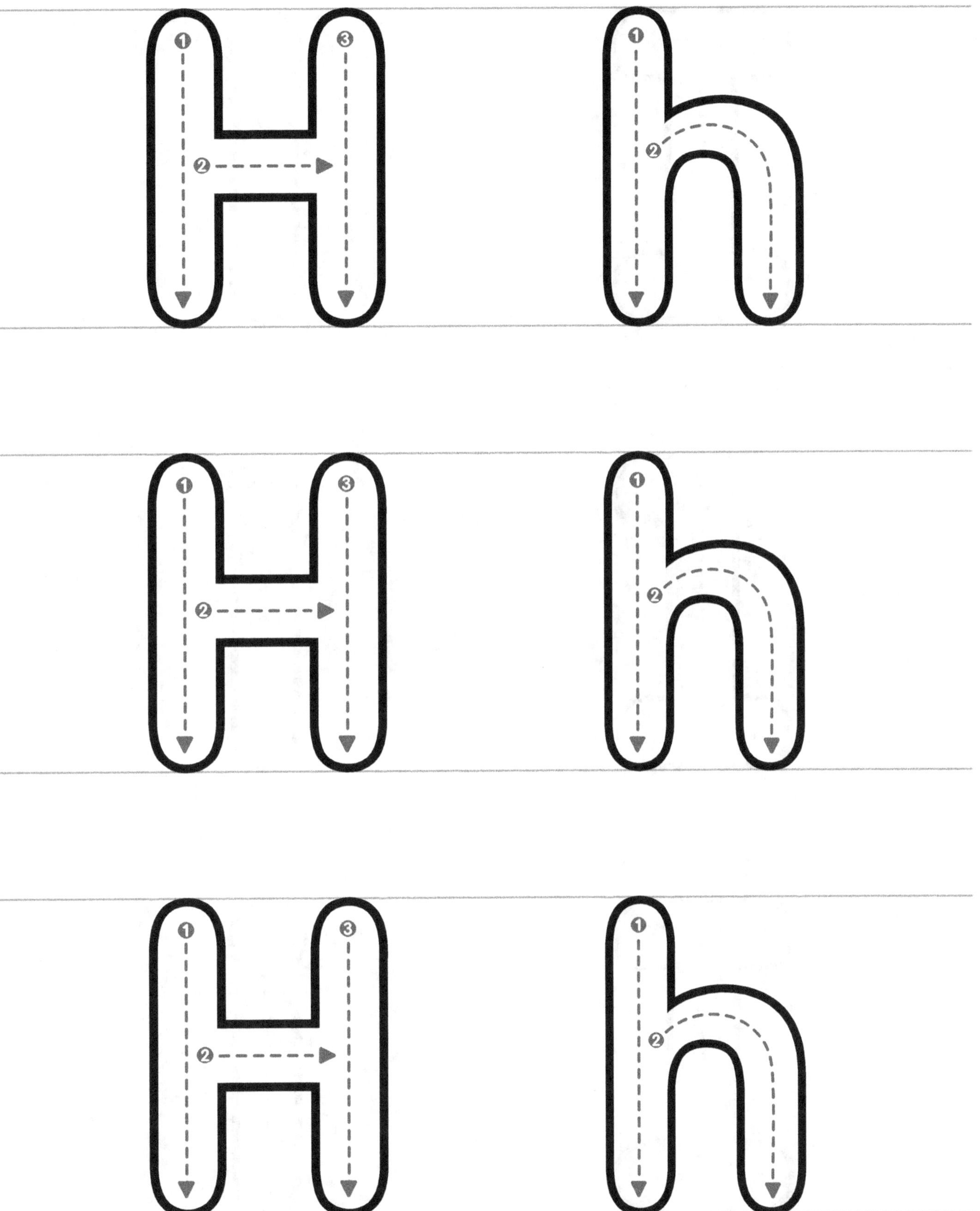

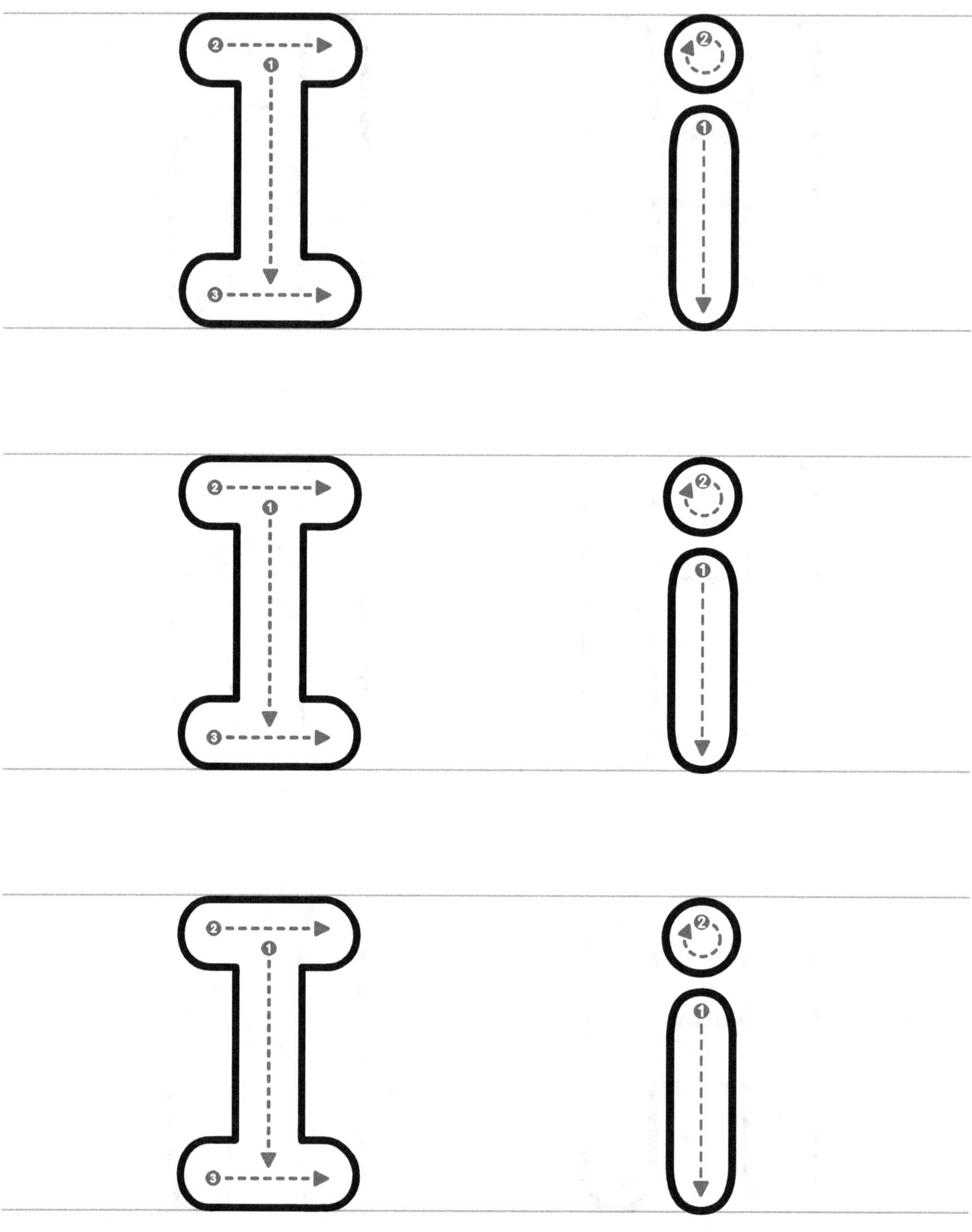

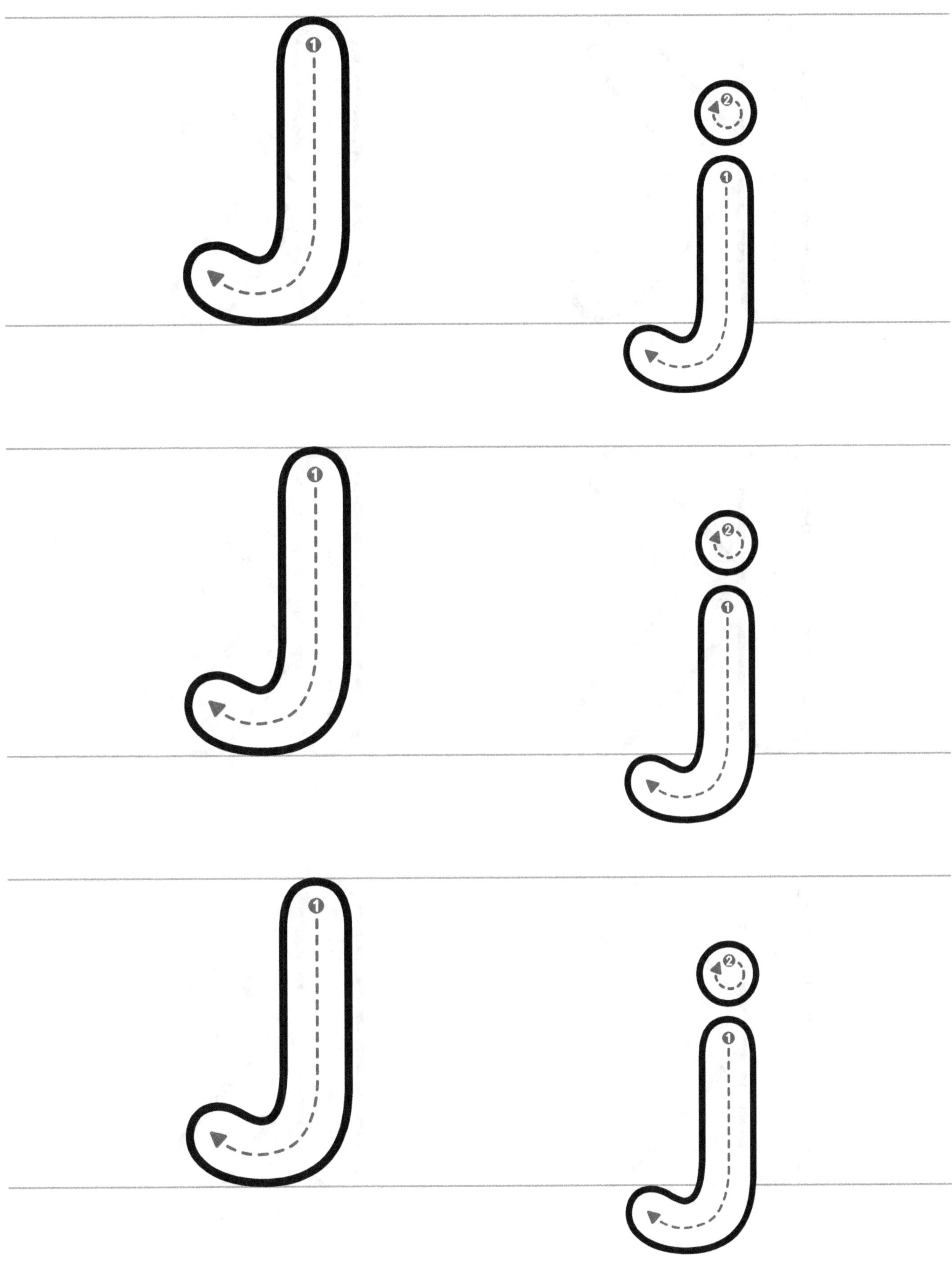

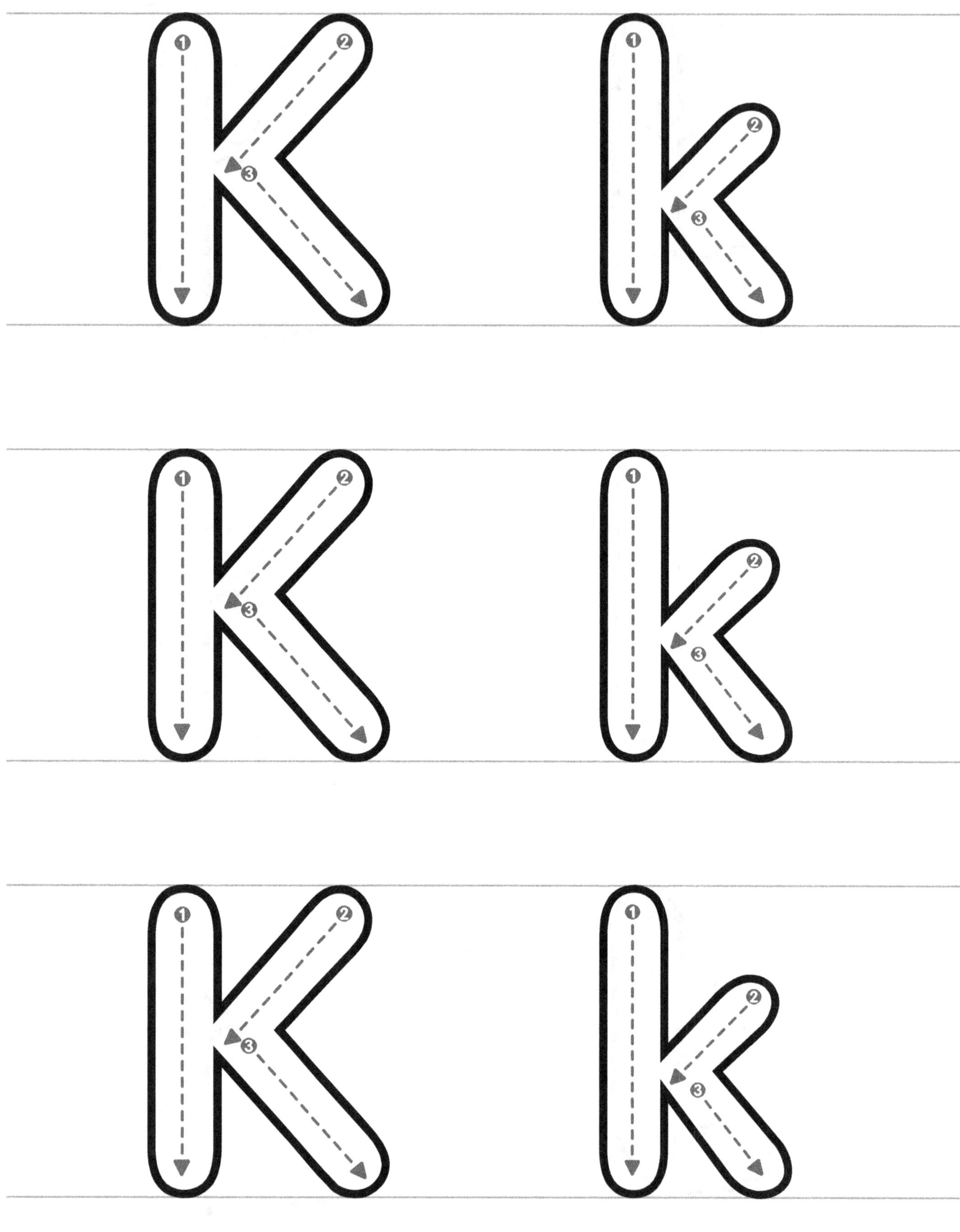

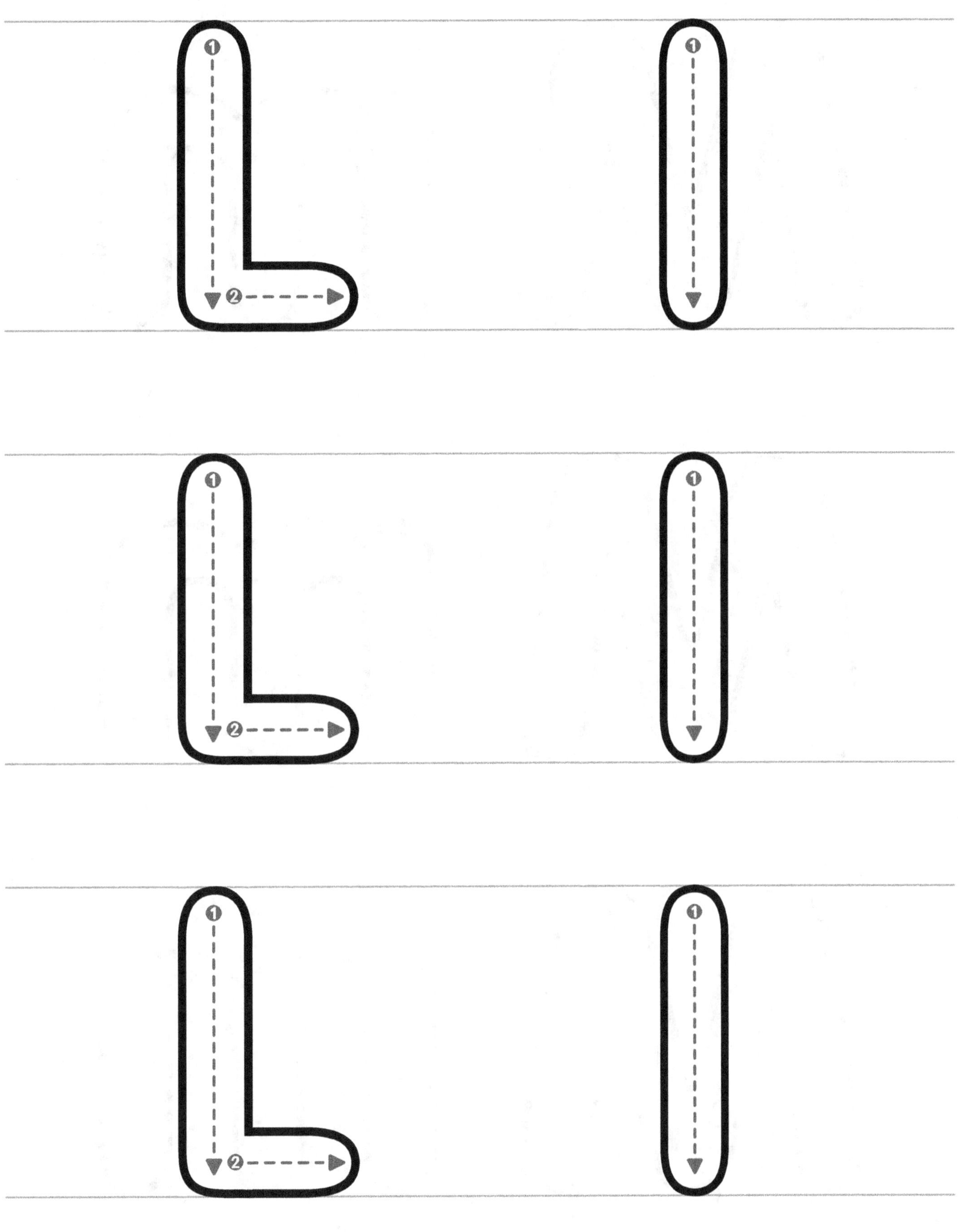

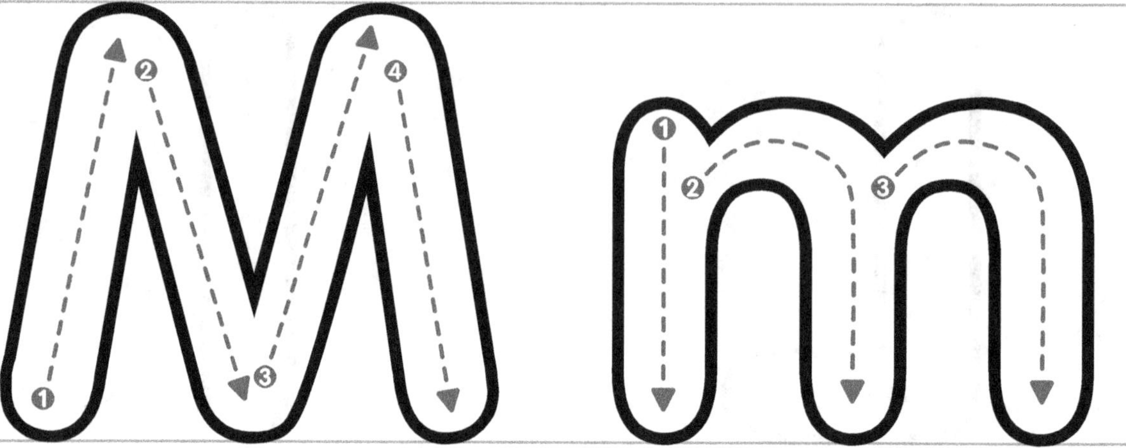

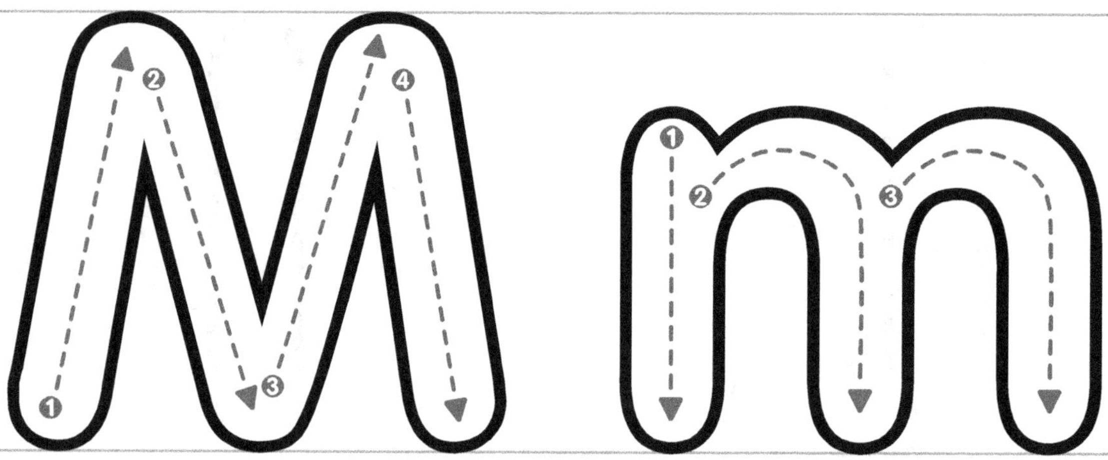

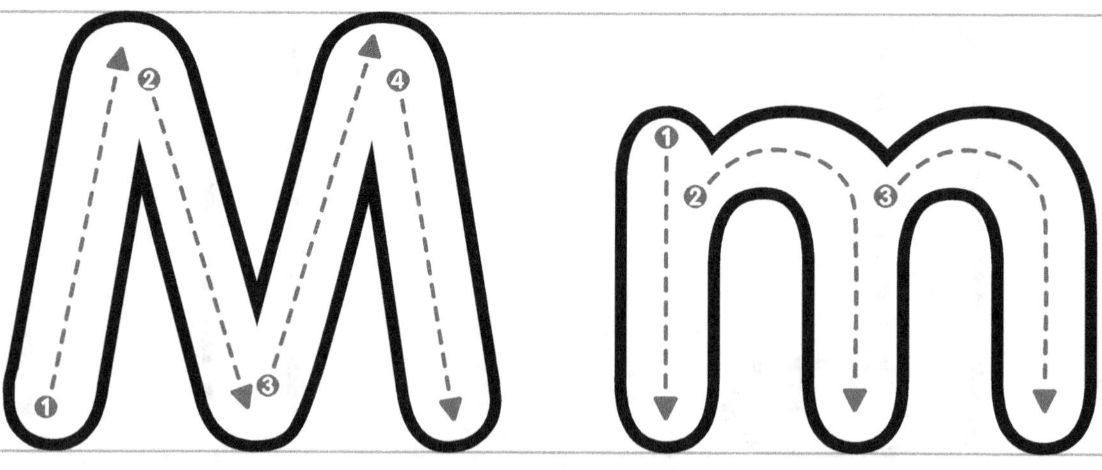

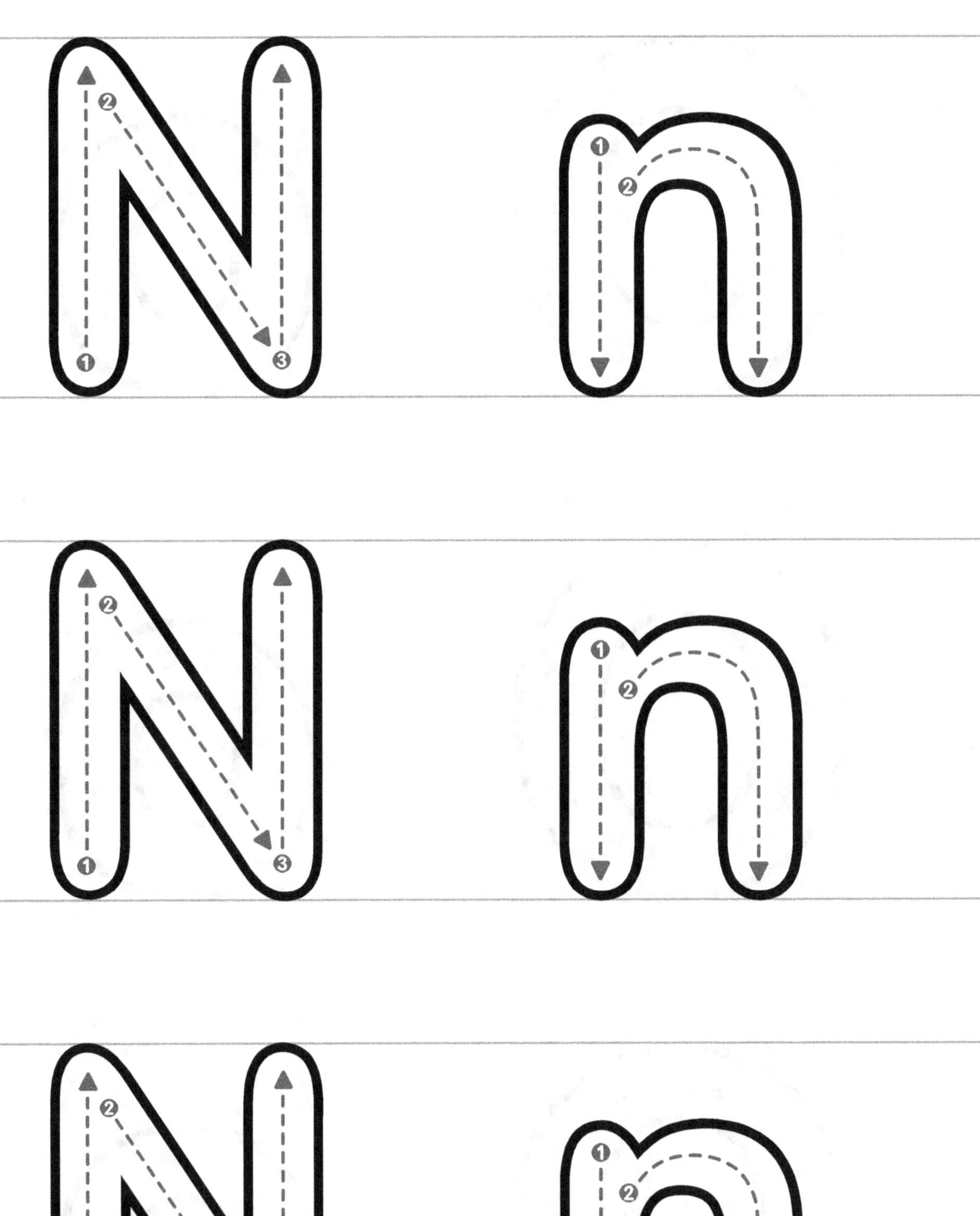

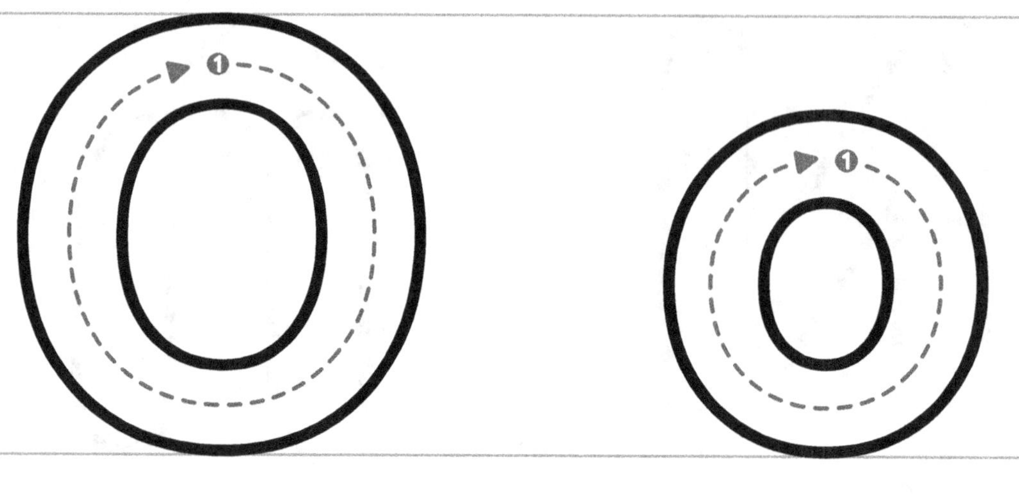

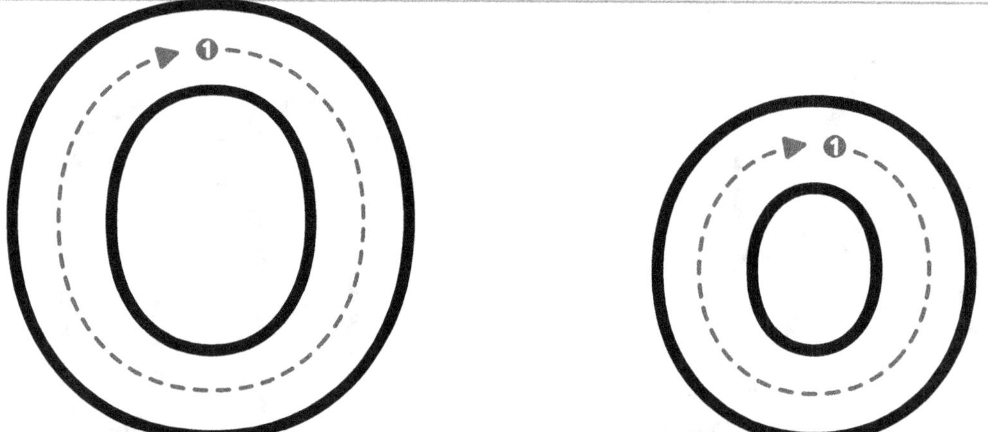

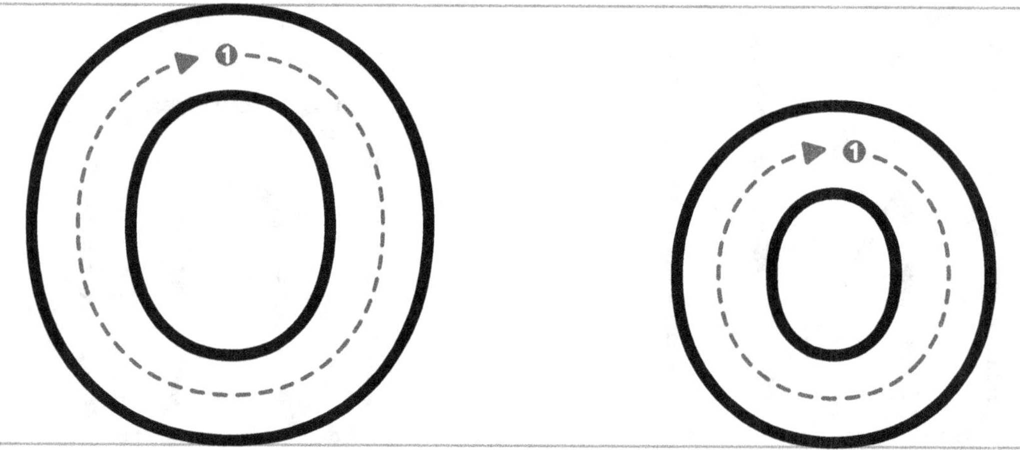

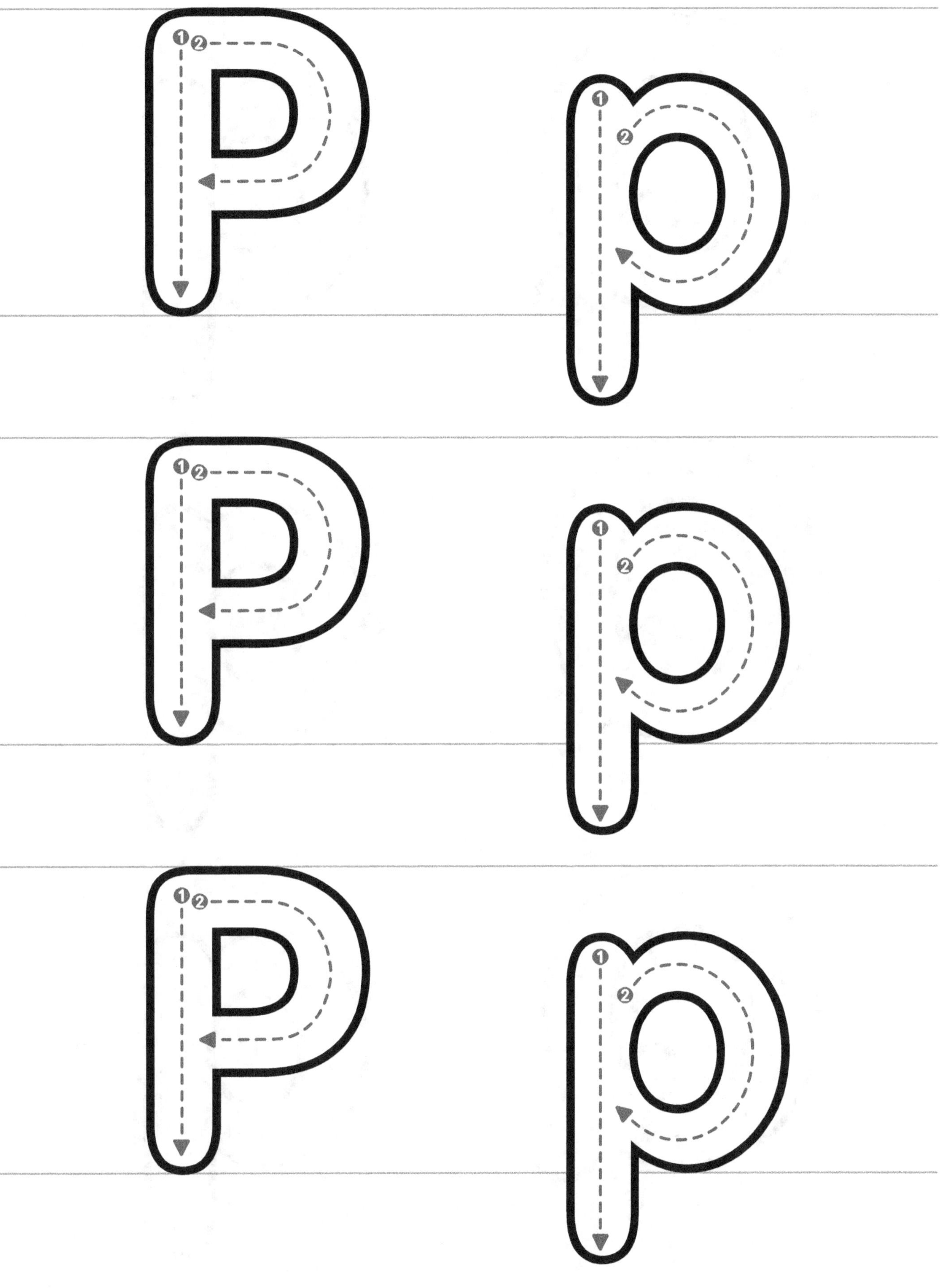

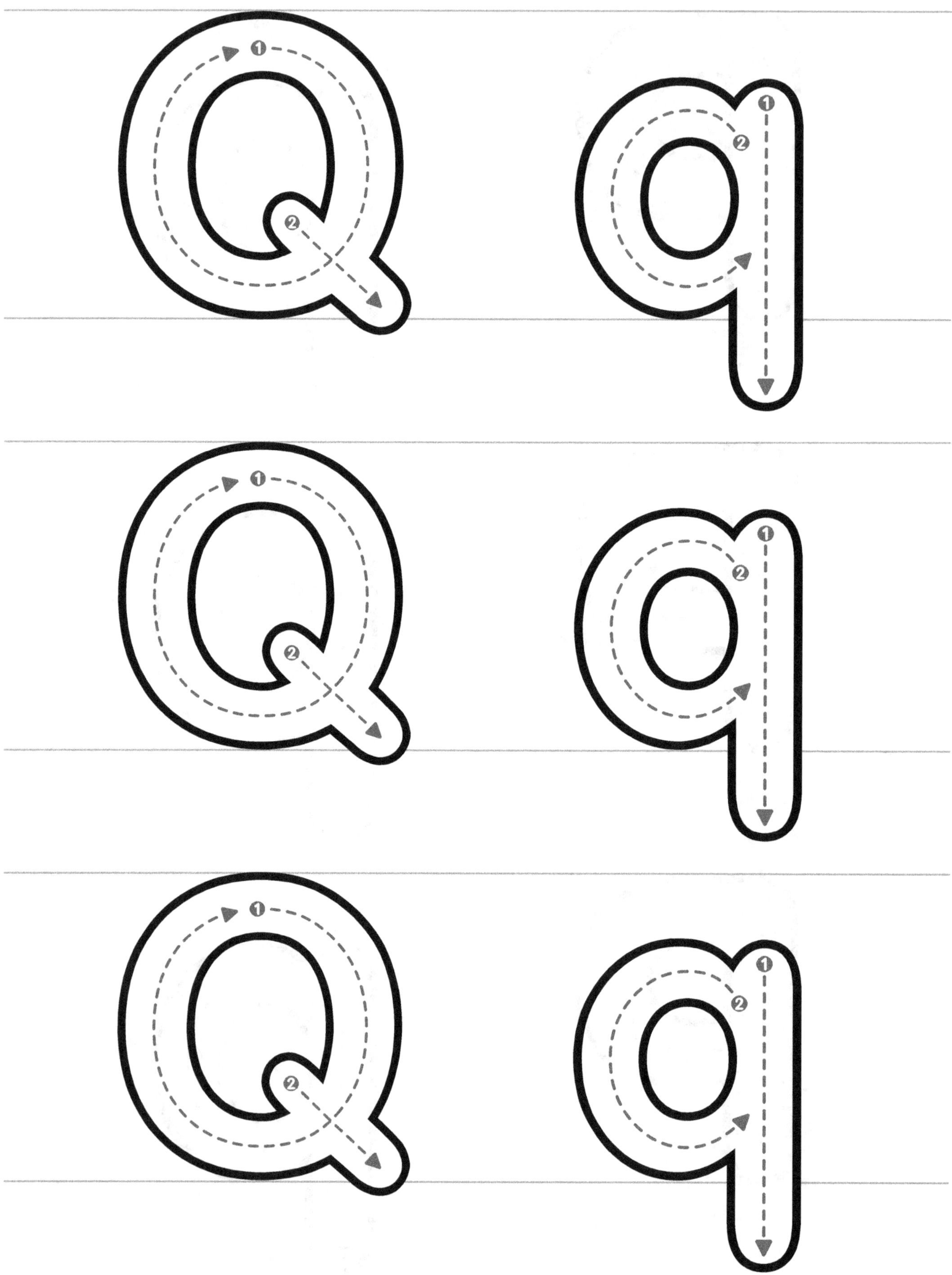

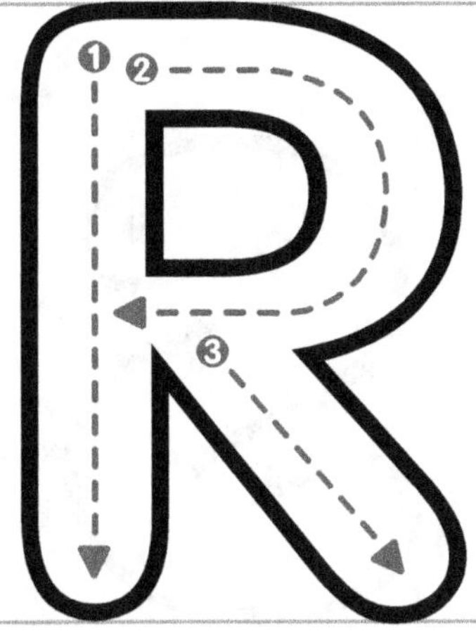 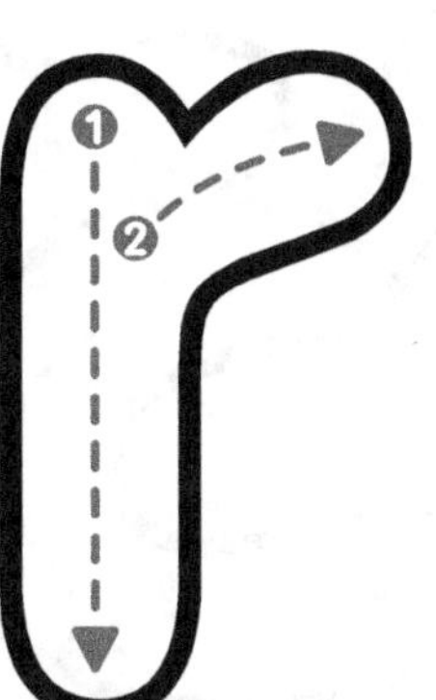

 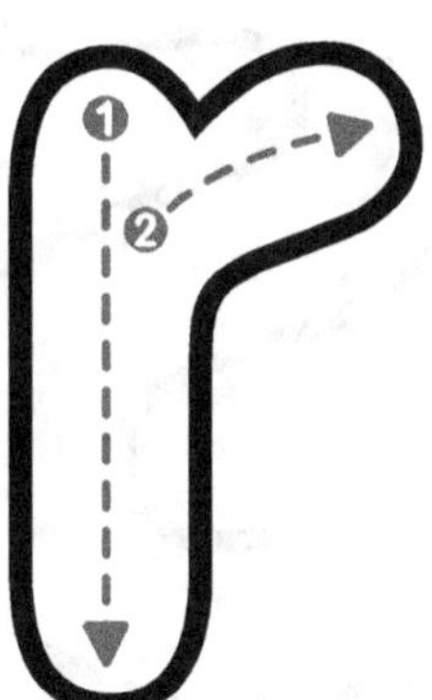

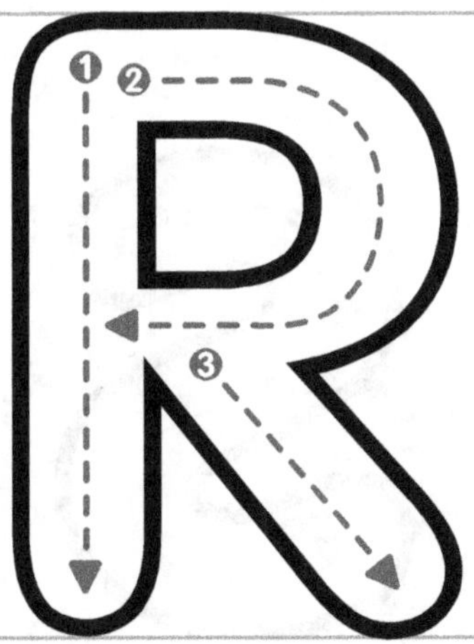 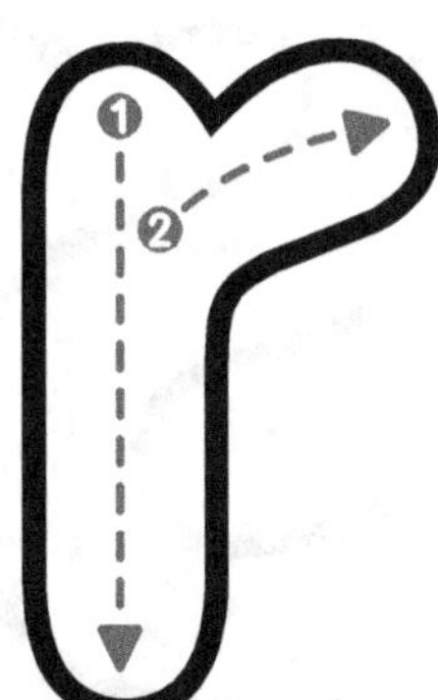

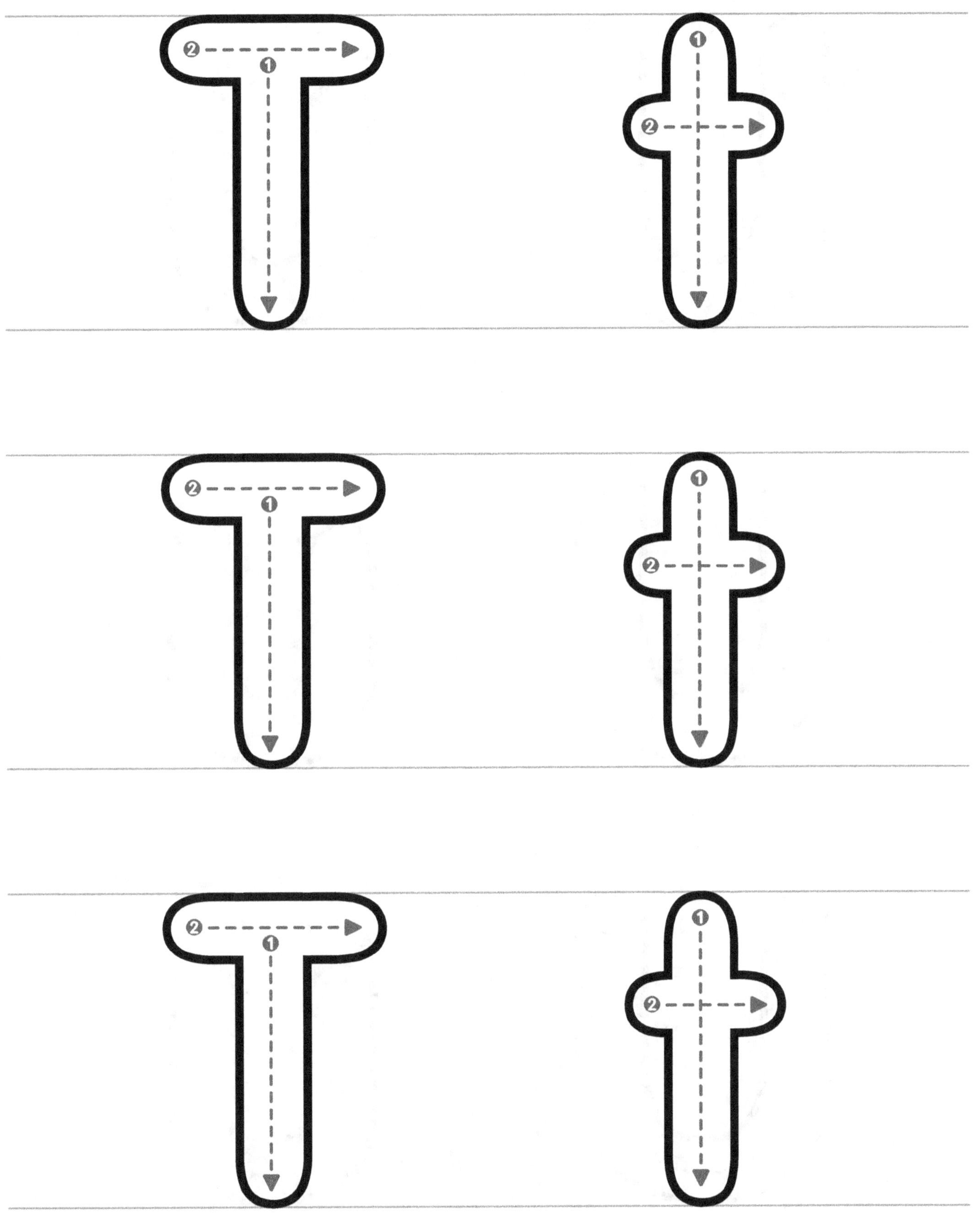

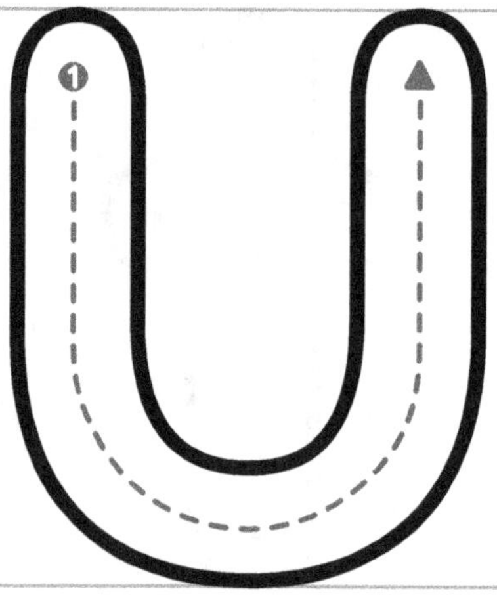
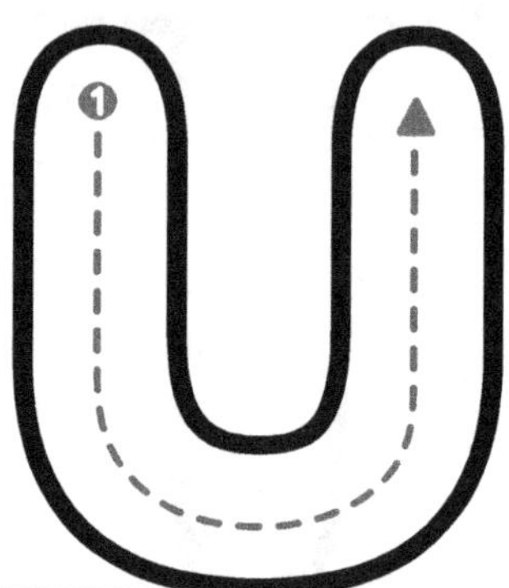
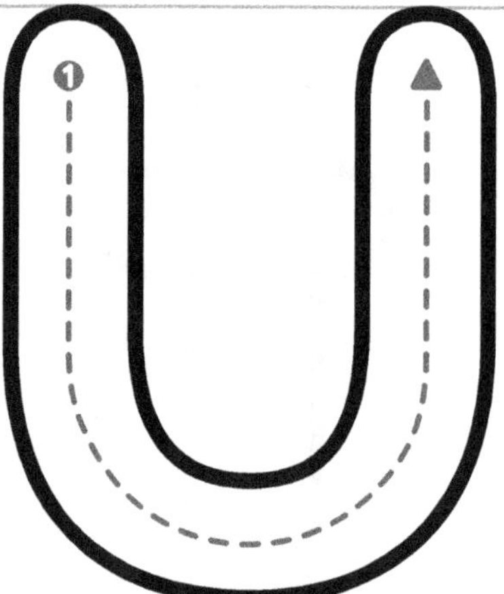
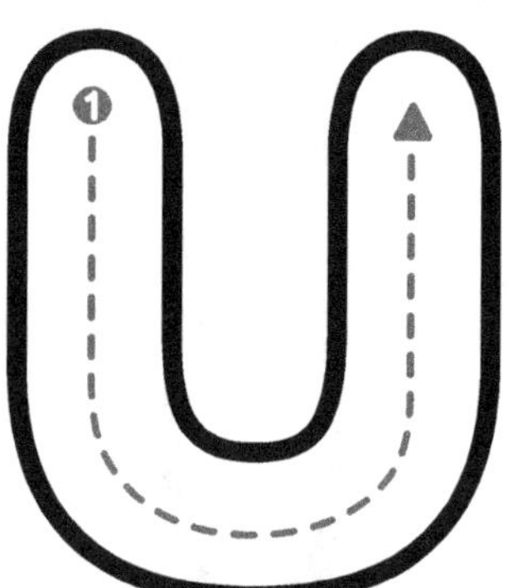
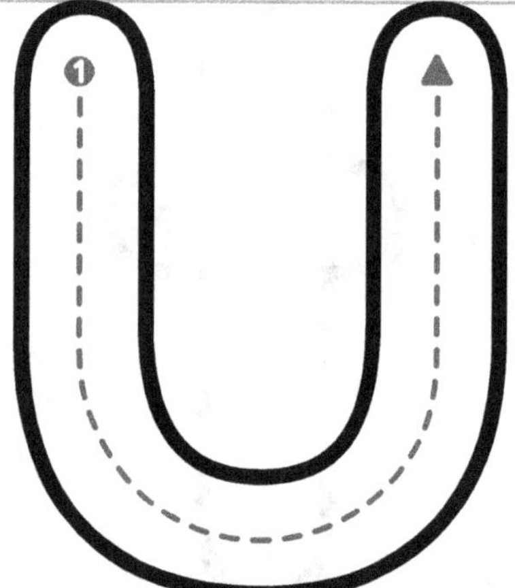
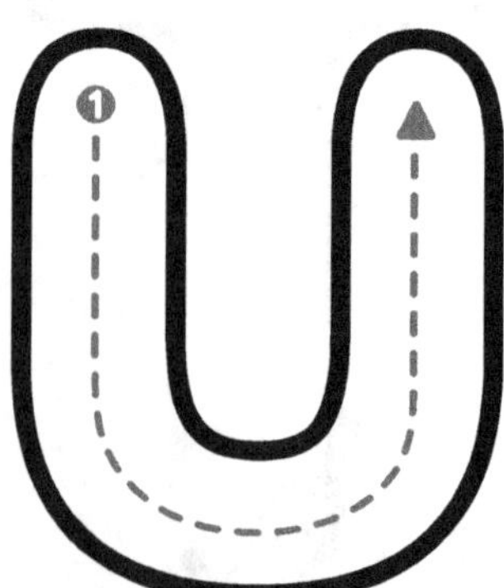

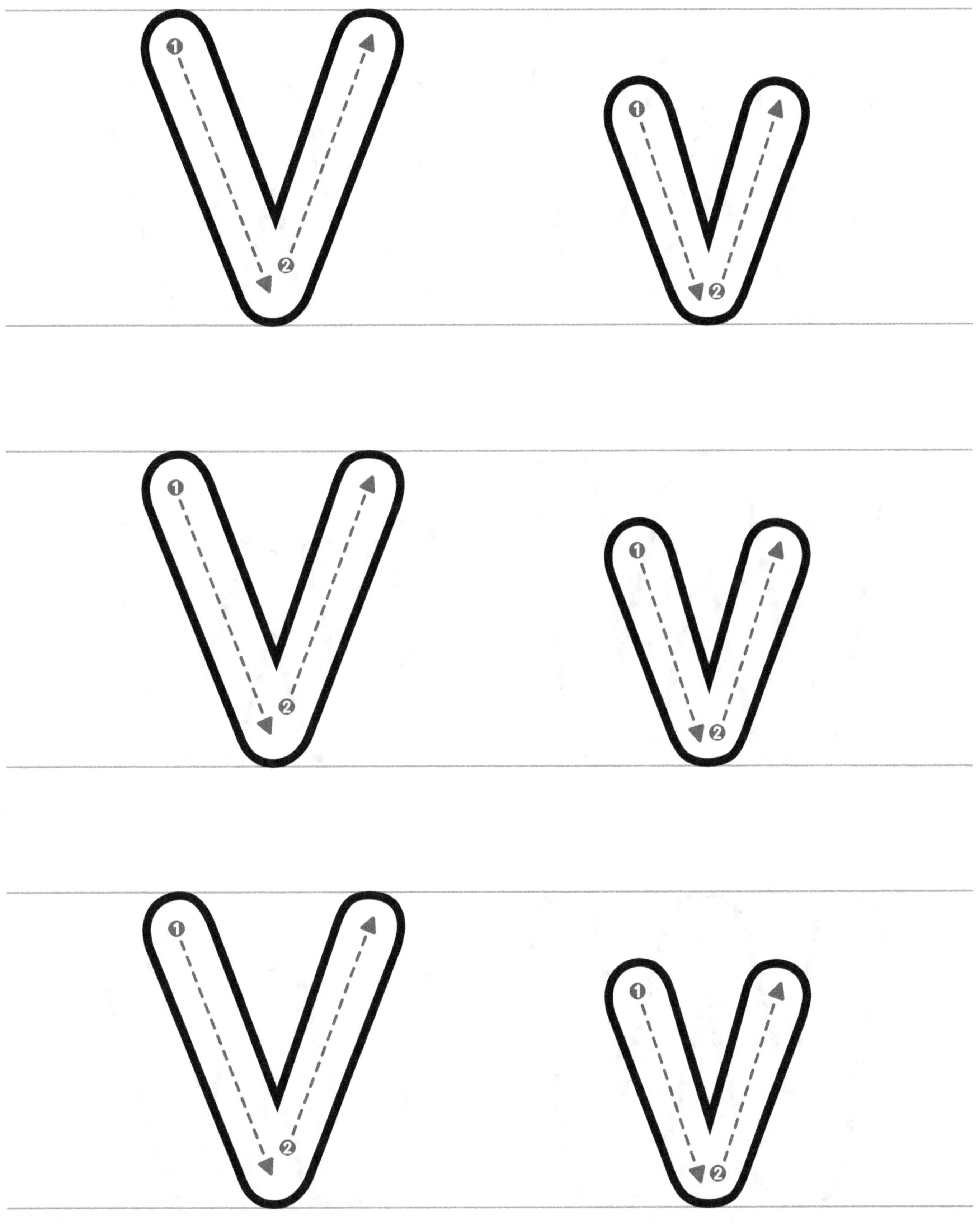

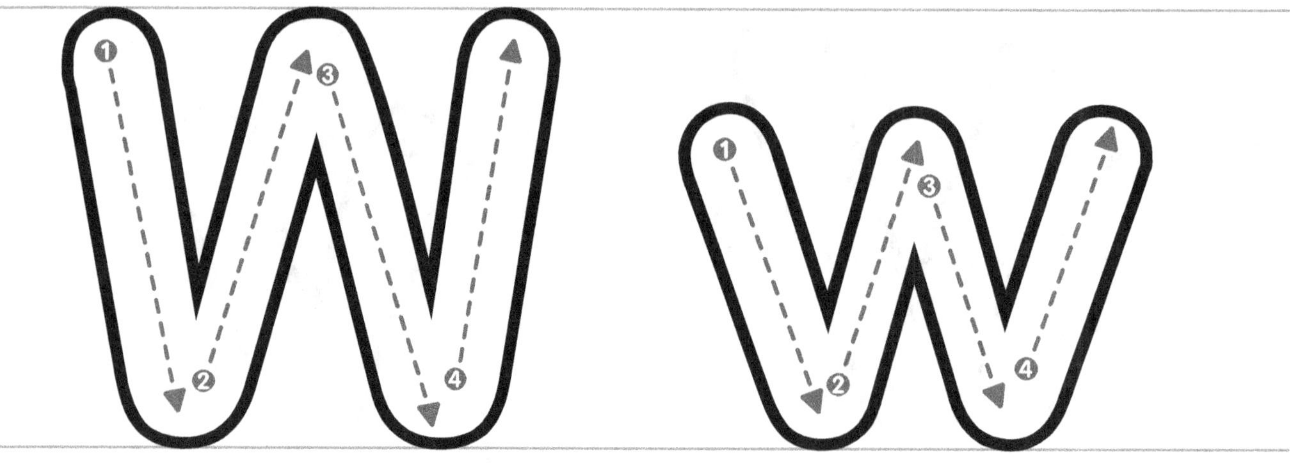

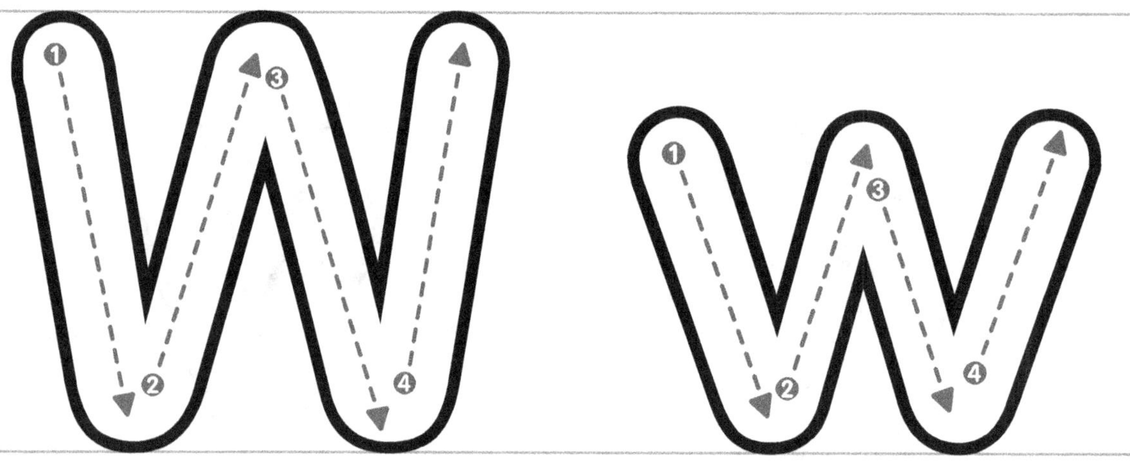

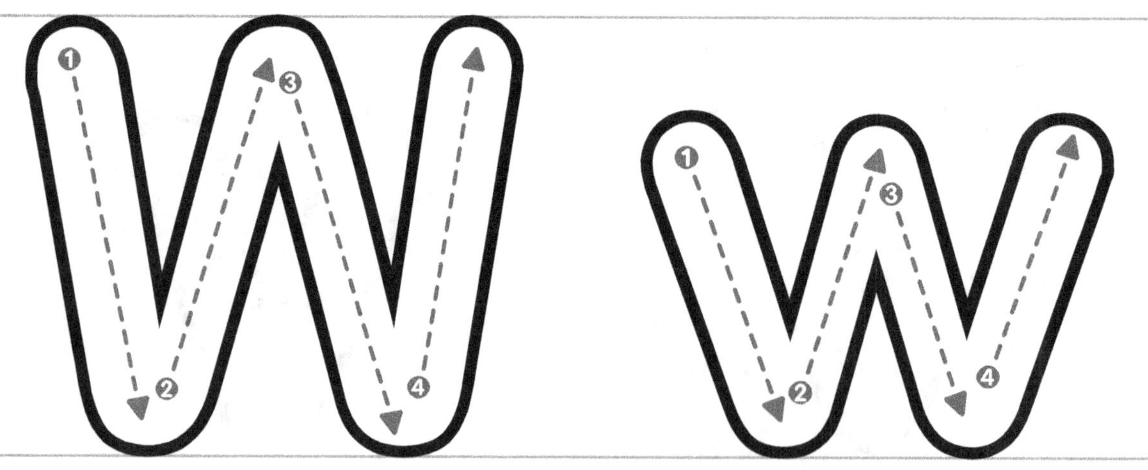

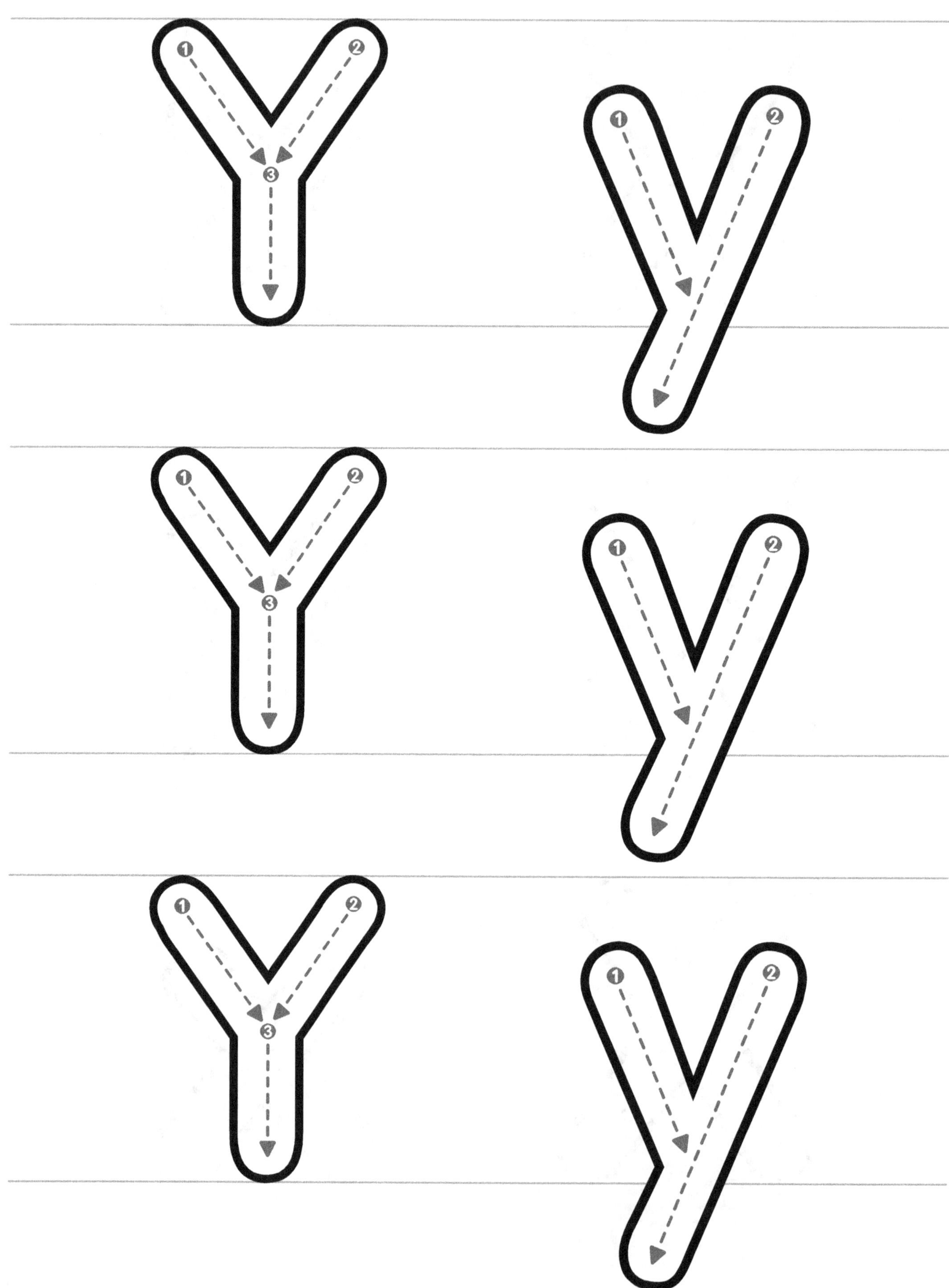

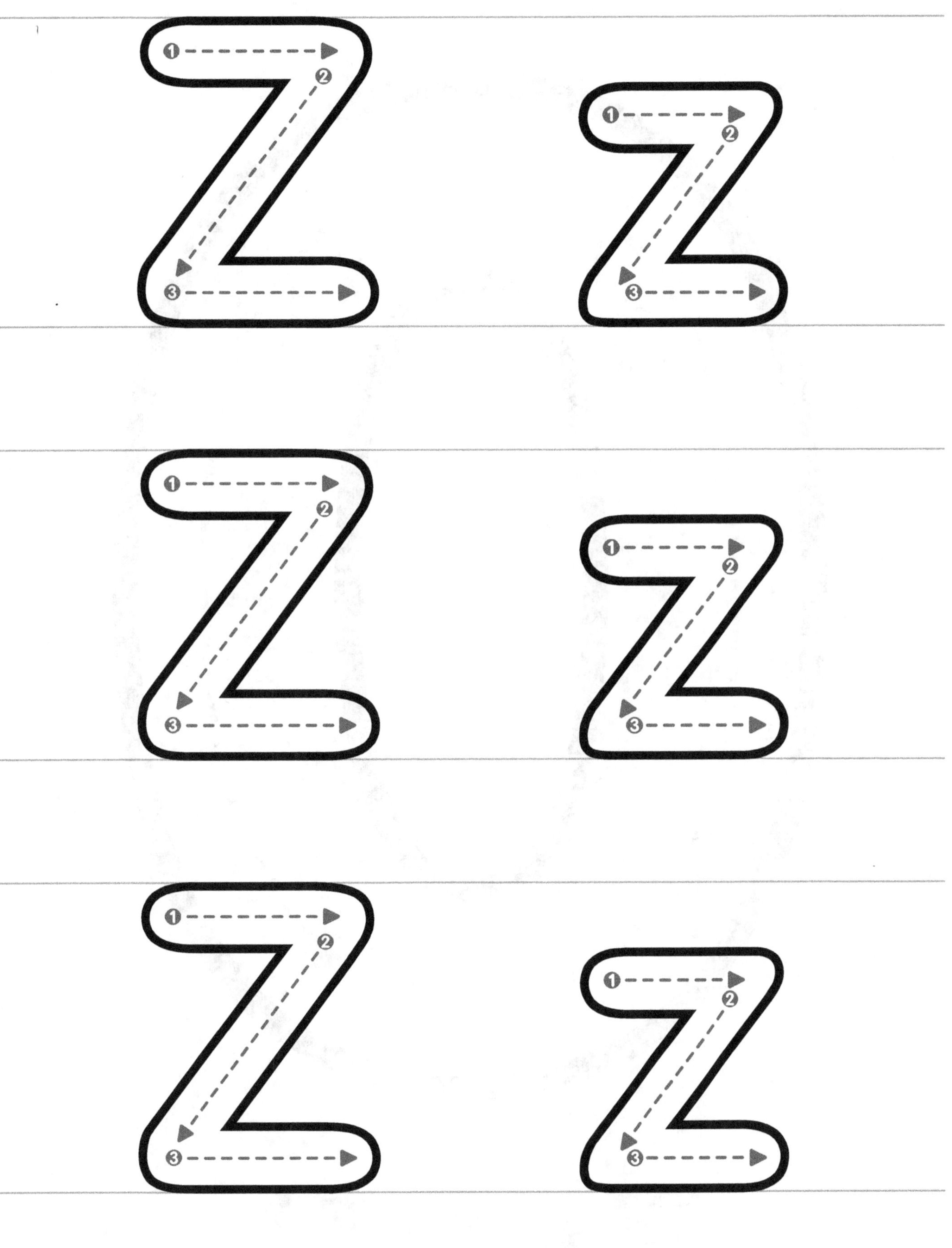

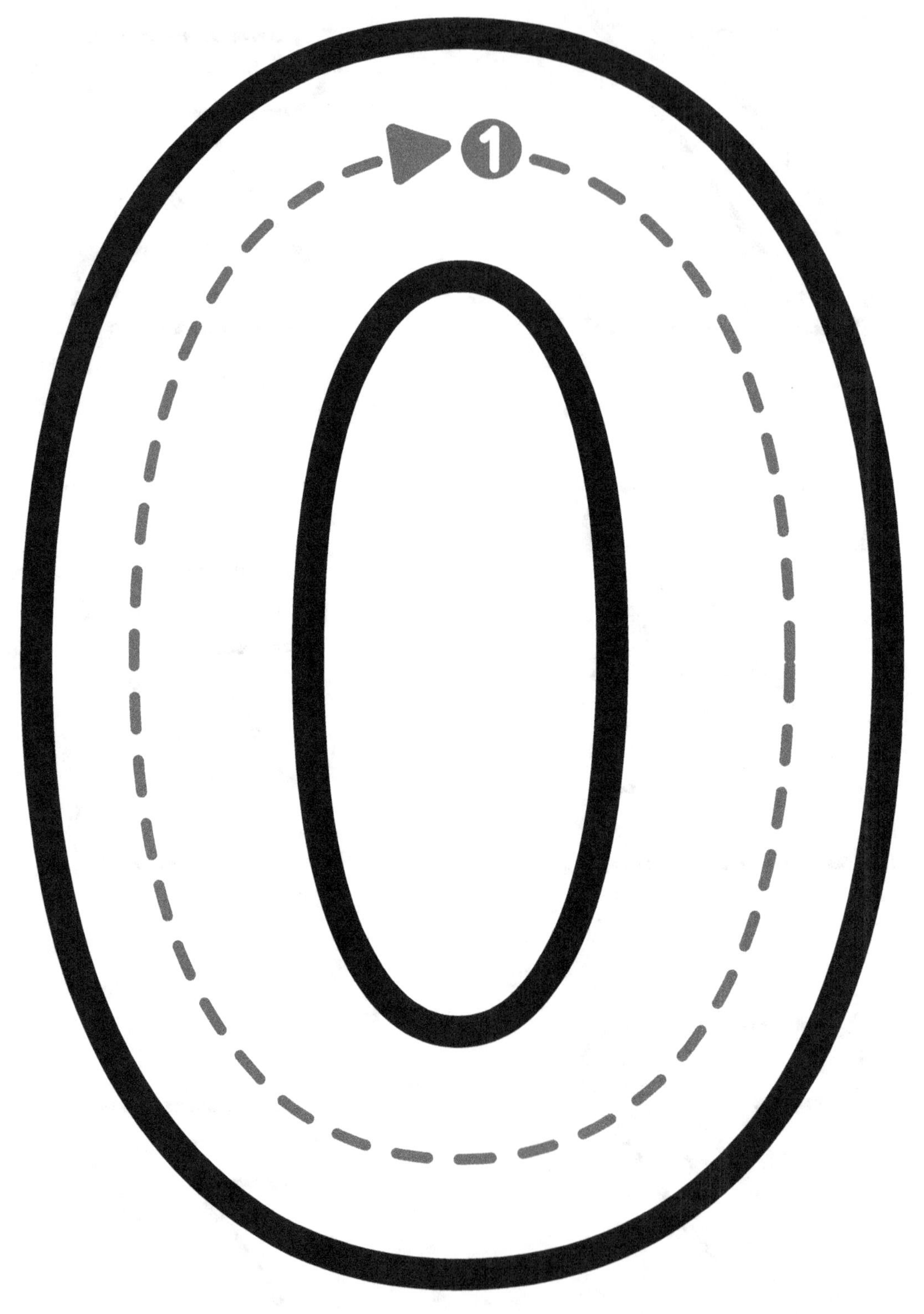

ZERO

1
2
ONE

TWO

THREE

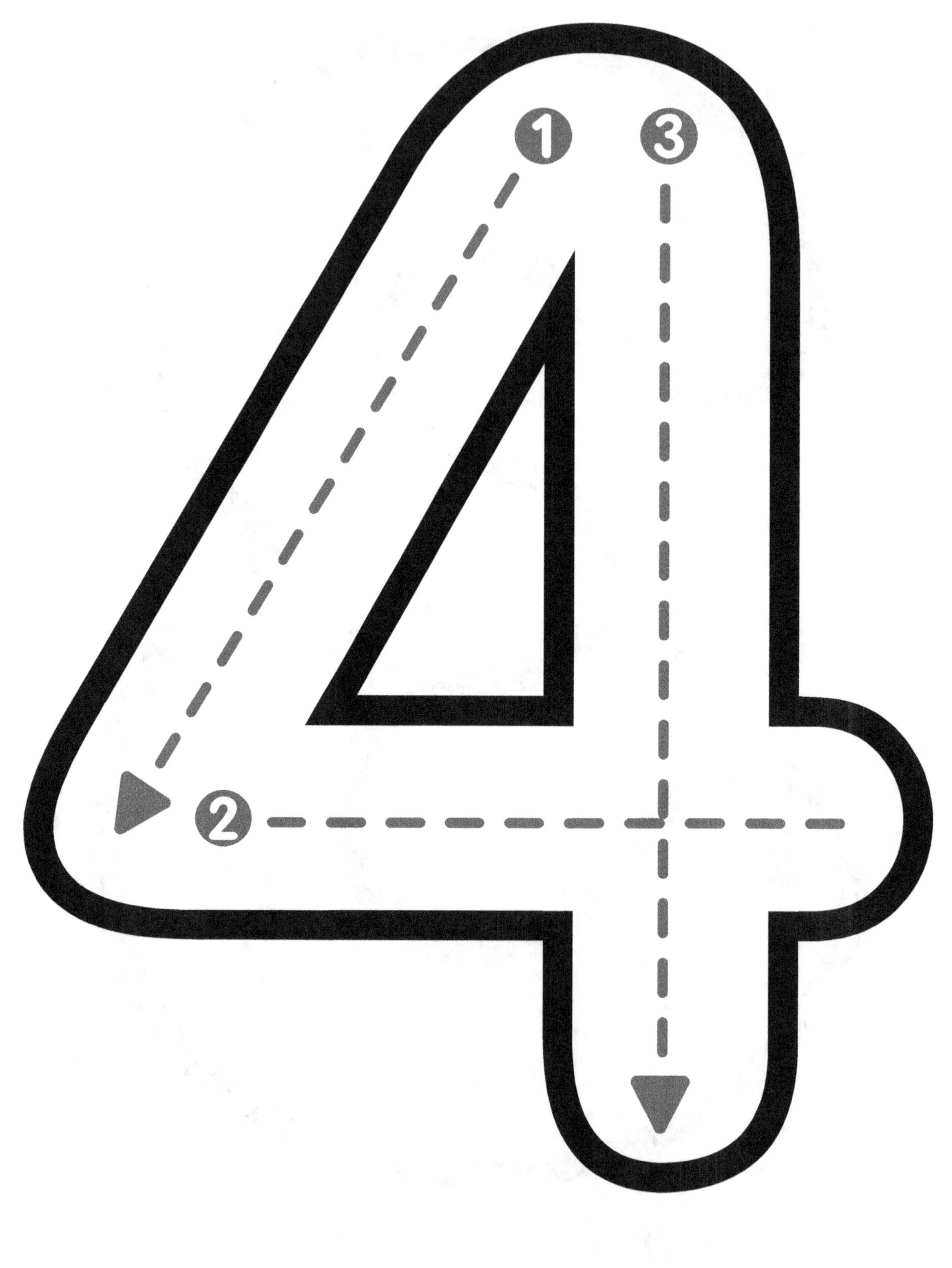

FOUR

FIVE

SIX

SEVEN

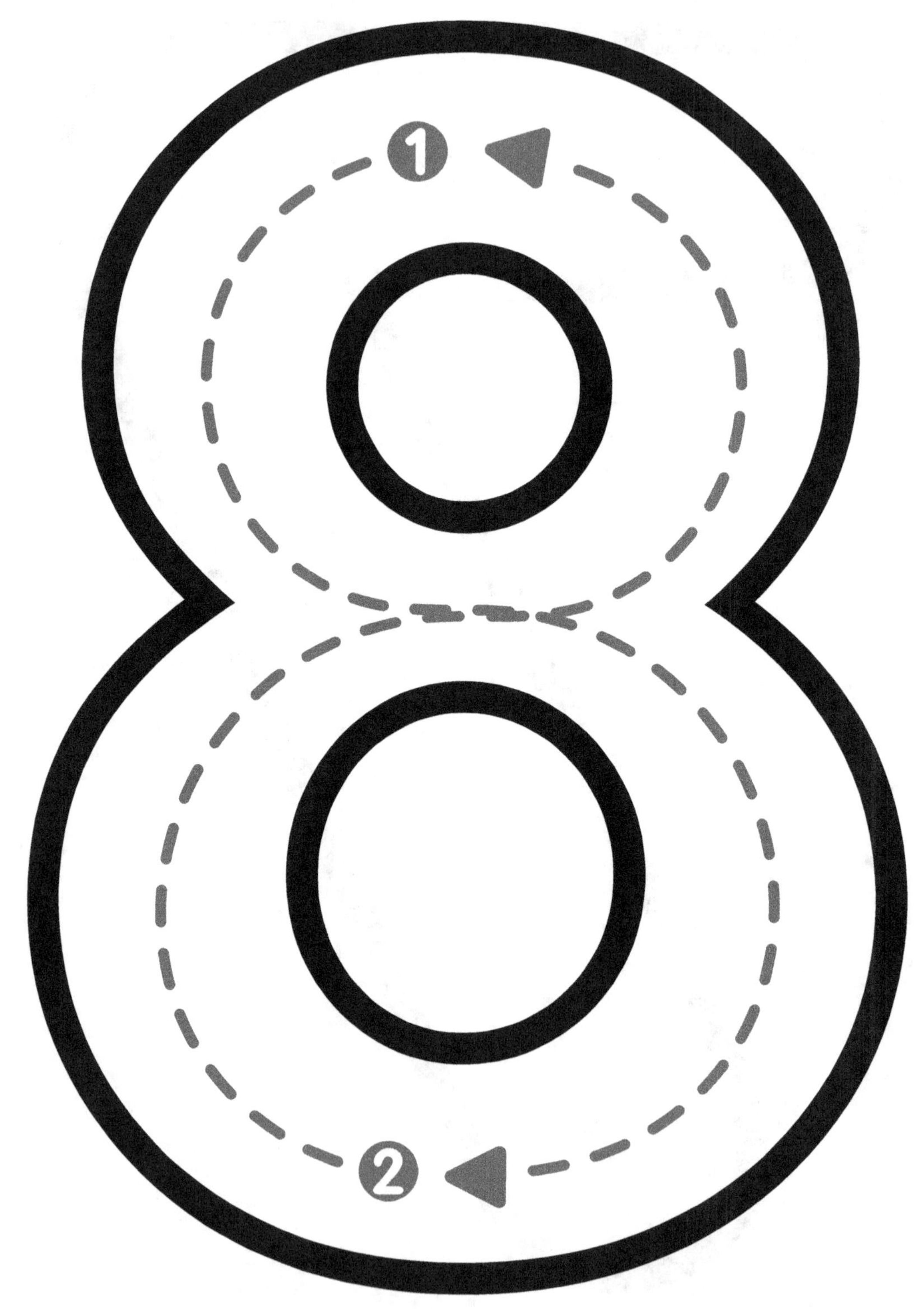

EIGHT

NINE